I Promise

I Promise

HOW 5 COMMITMENTS DETERMINE THE DESTINY OF YOUR MARRIAGE

DR. GARY SMALLEY

I Promise

Published by Integrity Publishers, a division of Integrity Media, Inc., 660 Bakers Bridge Avenue, Ste. 200, Franklin, TN 37067.

HELPING PEOPLE WORLDWIDE EXPERIENCE *the* MANIFEST PRESENCE *of* GOD.

Published in association with the literary agency of Result Source, Inc., 3651 Peachtree Pkwy., Suite 330, Suwanee, GA 30024 and the Gibson Group, 2085 Lakeshore Dr., Branson, MO 65616.

Cover Design: Christopher Tobias, Tobias' Outerwear for Books
Interior Design: Julie Whaley, Chickadee Design

ISBN-13: 9-781-59145-386-4 (hardcover)
ISBN-10: 1-59145-386-0 (hardcover)
ISBN-13: 9-781-59145-540-0 (international tradepaper)
ISBN-10: 1-59145-540-5 (international tradepaper)

Printed in the United States of America
06 07 08 09 10 BVG 9 8 7 6 5 4 3 2 1

This book is dedicated to the readers:
In all my years of writing and speaking to married couples around the world, I am always mindful that God has chosen my path. Not just the marriages I encounter that are hurting and struggling, but also the ones that are good but want to be great! So it is to you, my dear readers, that I so appreciate you taking the time to value this book. May you find great encouragement in the following pages and know that I'll be praying for you.

God's richest blessings in your marriages!
Gary

CONTENTS

ACKNOWLEDGMENTS

I wish to thank God first and foremost. Nothing I do could be accomplished without His wisdom, Word, and power.

And . . .

Thank you, Tom Williams, for all your patience and your gift of writing. God has truly blessed you with the gift of eloquence.

Thank you, Joey Paul, for having faith in me and guiding the entire project. Working with you is always a joy!

Many, many thanks to Dr. Greg Smalley who not only helped me understand this message, but helped me arrange it in this book. You are the best!

Thank you to Doug Slaybaugh and Buddy Owens for your faith in my message and the wonderful opportunity to work together. It was such a blessing to become friends and catch your passion for couples!

Also, my special appreciation goes to the many individuals at Purpose Driven Ministries that are behind the scenes—for doing their part in making this all happen.

A huge, big thank-you to my writing team—Terry Brown, Ted Cunningham, and Sue Parks—for keeping things flowing and for challenging me. Without you this book wouldn't have taken shape.

And just as important, thank you to my outstanding wife for being my constant cheerleader and dream maker. I love you, Norma!

I Promise

PART ONE

Security: The Secret to a Great Marriage

CHAPTER 1

Why Promise?

All husbands have experienced it. You are sleeping soundly when your wife shakes you awake and whispers: "Honey, I hear a noise downstairs. I think someone is in the house! Go check."

Begrudgingly you roll out of your warm bed, half asleep and a little irritated at having to check out what is sure to be yet another false alarm. But you dutifully set out to face whatever imagined evil is lurking downstairs. As usual, you find that it's a possum or some similar critter pattering on your porch. You mumble your findings to your wife and crawl back into bed, utterly oblivious to the fact that what has been a minor irritation to you is her greatest fear—the fear that she is not secure. Every husband on the planet has had this experience. I'm convinced that my main value in the marriage is to investigate noises and get rid of spiders.

At 4:20 a.m. on October 6, 2004, Norma's greatest fear materialized. Only this time I was out of town. She was alone.

It all started when the sound of glass breaking jolted her awake. She jumped out of bed and immediately checked to see if the bedroom door was locked. It was. Soon she heard more noises, first like the sound of someone screaming, then moments later something like the sound of an eerie chant. Norma was terrified.

Could it be Michael or Greg, she wondered. *Are my sons playing some kind of prank? If they are, I'll hurt them. This isn't funny.* "Please, Lord," Norma prayed under her breath, "Let this be a joke." But it certainly didn't have the feel of a joke.

And it wasn't. In the early morning hours a man had broken into our home. As we discovered later, he had over-dosed on methamphetamines and was having a drug- induced psychotic episode. (A year later he was sent to a criminal mental institute.)

This man had jumped off his sixteen-foot balcony and shattered his ankle. He limped across the street, dragging his foot behind him, and crashed through our garage window falling hard on the glass and debris and cutting himself severely. But he felt no pain because of the methamphetamines. Bleeding profusely, he broke through the garage door and entered our home. He was convinced that demons were out to kill him as he careened through our house, knocking over furniture and wrecking our decor. From where Norma hid, the noise seemed deafening. She was sure that he would find her; it was simply a matter of time.

As fear tightened its grip on her, she instinctively did the exact thing TV talk show hosts had taught her. She ran into the bathroom and locked herself in the toilet area. The intruder would have to break through three heavy doors to get her. Norma then dialed 911. (I am so thankful that we followed through on installing a phone in our bathroom!) Within three minutes a police officer arrived, but he couldn't enter our home because he wasn't sure how many people were inside. He needed backup. So he waited in our driveway for additional officers to show up.

Meanwhile, Norma endured twenty minutes of this man screaming, chanting, and destroying our stuff—the longest twenty minutes of her life. Several times she heard him screaming so close that she was terrified that he was about to burst through the door into our bedroom. "He's coming in, he's coming in," she cried to the 911 operator. The operator reassured Norma that the police were ready to burst in if he actually entered the bedroom. Ultimately the deranged man barricaded himself against his demons inside the closet of a second floor bedroom—the room right above Norma.

When the police finally apprehended this man, they found blood on the door handle of our bedroom. He had ventured all the way to our bedroom door, but for some reason he had stopped. Norma believes to this day that God's angels stood there with their hands outstretched, telling him that he could go no further.

On that October night, Norma's worst fears were realized. She thought she was secure in our home because we had a state-of-the-art home security system. The only problem was that the system had not been activated that night. We had this first-rate security system, but we paid little attention to using it because we never suspected we would need it. Why would we? Our little town of Branson, Missouri, has little or no crime. It never occurred to us that someone very sick was living right across the street. We thought we were secure, but we were not. Immediately I promised to install additional security measures and vowed that I would never again neglect punching in the security code to our system. That promise was extremely important, but I'll get back to that shortly. First I want to address the importance of security.

Our Need for Security

You may have a similar security failure in your marriage—one that you are blissfully unaware of, or one just waiting to happen. Just so there's no misunderstanding here, I'm not talking about physical security. That's important, and you need to take care of it; but it's another issue entirely. The breach of security in our home that threatened Norma is merely an analogy to the kind of security you need in your marriage. What I'm talking about here is emotional security—the security to truly open up and be known at a deep, intimate level without fear of being blamed, criticized, judged, or condemned. Like most couples, you may think that a successful marriage depends on relationship skills—how many you possess, how well developed they are, and how successful you are in applying them. But none of these skills will have any effect if your marriage lacks that one, basic, foundational ingredient—security.

One of my dreams when I established our ministry's research center was to find out what is really necessary for couples to thrive in their marriages. After directing a research team in years of study, my son, Dr. Greg Smalley, has determined that the number one key to a satisfying, intimate marriage is for couples to maintain security.

Security is the unsung need, the overlooked ingredient that can make your marriage the best on the face of the earth. Security underscores and supports every facet of your relationship. Security makes your marriage feel like the safest place on earth, the place where you want to live and grow and love. But to experience that level of security, you must build a sound relational security system and punch in the code to activate it. When those uneasy feelings between the two of you begin to go away, you'll be on your way to the best marriage you can imagine.

Research has convinced me that security is the primary key to a great marriage.

Why is security the key to a great marriage?

UCLA neuroscientist, Dr. Allan Shore, writes that all humans desire satisfying relationships, because a section of our brain has been hardwired to seek a loving connection with others. The need for relationship is built in. It's part of the innate nature of every human on earth. Think about it: all your life you've been trying to connect to best friends, parents, siblings, a mate, etc. But regardless of how hard a person may try, deep, emotionally-based, intimate, best-friend-type of relationships only happen when you feel safe and secure in the presence of the other.

Dr. Bob Paul, director of the National Marriage Institute, calls this concept feeling "safe."[1] Dr. Paul has discovered that when you feel safe, you automatically open up and share more and more of your deepest self. As you continue opening up, the best-friend relationship begins to happen naturally. Close your eyes and imagine living with a mate who completely accepts you for who you are. He never tries to change you. She is constantly looking for clues to understand you better. He not only highly values who you are, but is fascinated by your every move, every word, every thought. Would that be great or what?

Most married couples are continually on the lookout for ways to create that kind of intimate experience. Typical strategies that we often explore to create intimacy might include: learning about each other's love language and emotional needs; being attentive to romantic gestures and events, like sending flowers, cards, and planning candlelight dinners; maintaining regular date nights; attending church or relationship conferences; developing great sex techniques; reading marriage books; or joining a small group and talking about your marriage. And the strategy list can go on and on and on.

Don't get me wrong. I'm not knocking these avenues of marriage improvement. After all, I've written some about these techniques myself in other books. Knowing your mate's love language, for example, is a great strategy after your marriage feels secure. In fact, it can help create more safety. But most of the books I've written, as well as many of the books of my author friends, outline strategies for *enhancing* your marriage relationship after the vital element of security between partners is established. While on some level these strategies are worthwhile and helpful, our marriage research center found that they don't work well to produce intimacy unless couples first build a foundation of security into their marriage.

Security will never happen in any marriage until partners get over their natural resistance to openness with each other. Why do we have this resistance? Because openness makes us vulnerable, and vulnerability means risk. We're not quite sure what our spouse will say or do when we truly open up, or how he or she may use what we reveal. *What will he think when I dare to reveal this long-hidden truth about myself? What will she say when I tell her what I've done? Will he laugh or ridicule me when I reveal to him what I'm thinking?* When you risk you can lose. And when the risk involves the impairment of a vital relationship, the loss can be devastating. This is why so many marriage partners pull back from connection and intimacy. Usually it's an attempt to avoid being hurt, humiliated, embarrassed, or simply being made uncomfortable by the prospect of complete openness. We have a natural tendency to avoid risk.

The way to overcome this risk is to establish in your marriage the security of knowing that each of you can safely reveal your heart to the other without fear of condemnation. The only way to achieve this kind of marital intimacy is to focus significant time, attention, and energy into creating an environment in which both partners feel secure in each other's love and acceptance when they make themselves vulnerable by opening up. Security reduces the risk. Just think how simple this can be: you don't have to be the expert relationship guru, mastering all the strategies and techniques designed to enhance intimacy; all you need is to feel secure in your marriage, and the best relationship possible will happen naturally. Is that great news or what?

We spend so much needless energy trying to hide. We put up walls to obscure our inner selves and try to project the image we think our mates want so that when they look at us through their camera lens, they will like what they see. But by putting up that façade, we tend to keep parts of ourselves closed and protected. We may ignore or deny how we actually feel. We may draw on a whole host of behaviors to avoid relational risks—behaviors such as getting angry, defensive, or demanding—as a way of distracting our mate from our own vulnerability or deflecting his or her condemnation. Unfortunately, these strategies usually limit the quality of intimacy in our marriage because it's hard for the other to get close to us if we're standing behind a thick wall. We hide because we don't feel the security to be open, and openness is a must in satisfying marriage relationships.

In spite of the risks, the potential benefits of an intimate marriage are many. Intimacy creates the ideal opportunity to:

- love deeply and be loved;
- experience a significant sense of belonging;
- have a clearer sense of purpose in life;
- have the ability to make a major difference in another's life;
- and have a way of fully expressing the best of who we are.

In your marriage, do you feel secure enough to open up and share who you really are, including your deepest thoughts, hopes, and dreams without those uneasy feelings creeping in—feelings that maybe you'll be blamed, criticized, condemned, judged, or ridiculed? Do you fear that your heart will be broken into and your feelings wrecked or your dreams crushed? Do you feel that you must barricade your heart and protect your innermost self behind locks and doors because your mate will not give you the security of being open?

Ever since she was a little girl, Heather's first ambition was to be a mother. But due to taking care of her own invalid mother, she did not marry Troy until she was almost thirty. Troy worked as a fireman, but he was very good with his hands and had a real talent for fine cabinetwork. He often dreamed of starting his own cabinet business. Heather also worked, and so they had put aside a pretty good nest egg. Troy hoped to use the money to open his cabinet shop. Heather knew of Troy's dream, but she wanted to start their family soon, and they would need that money for expenses when their household no longer had two incomes. For a long time Heather could not bring herself to tell Troy that she was concerned that she could hear her biological clock ticking, and if they didn't start their family soon it would be too late.

One evening after dinner she said to him, "Honey, have I ever told you how much I want us to have a family?"

"Well, I figured you wanted kids," Troy responded. "And as soon as we get my business off the ground, we'll do what it takes to make that happen."

"That may be too late," Heather replied. "We really need to start our family now or it may not happen."

Troy knew that what she said was true. He also heard the warmth in her voice as she spoke of having a child. He wanted his cabinet shop, but he also loved his wife. So instead of putting her off, he started asking her all kinds of questions about her hopes and dreams. How many children did she want? Did she intend to quit work after the baby came? What did having babies cost these days? What kind of lifestyle would she settle for if they didn't have as much money as they had planned? Troy's interest in her dreams and the sincerity of his questions led Heather to open up and reveal her innermost feelings about how important family was to her.

She was sensitive to his dreams as well, and as they talked things out he decided cabinet making would make a great hobby. The tools and equipment would cost only a fraction of the huge expense of opening a shop. And with his string of days off as a fireman, he would have enough time to take on small orders and make considerable extra money without sacrificing family time. And who knows? Maybe in time he could build his shop.

"Okay, let's have that baby as soon as possible. In fact," Troy said, grinning, "why don't we go upstairs and start right now?"

Wouldn't it be great to live with someone who really wants you to share everything about yourself? Wouldn't it be great to have a husband or wife who is excited about discovering who you are, what you believe, how you think, why you do what you do, what you dream, and what makes you tick? Wouldn't it make you feel secure to have someone who actually enjoys getting to know you and enjoys it when you change or mature? That's security.

Creating Security Is Easier than You Think

If you are like me, you long for a marriage in which you feel completely secure in your mate's love. You want to feel safe and free to open up and reveal who you really are and know that your partner will still love, accept, and value you—no matter what you say or who you are. It can happen, and it may be easier than you think.

When you think about it, openness is really the default setting for human beings. We are, by nature, inclined to be open. No state of being takes less energy to maintain than openness, because it involves just relaxing and being you. Maintaining defenses, walls, and fortresses against your mate takes tremendous energy. Projecting images to get your spouse to see you a certain way, or to like or accept you, requires a huge amount of work. Simply being and expressing who you are does not. It follows that couples who feel truly secure in their marriage can chuck these masks and facades and use their energy to live and enjoy life.

When married couples live together in a state of openness, intimacy naturally occurs. Let me elaborate on that. Intimacy is the experience of being close to your mate and openly sharing information—either about yourself or some topic relating to you—with the confidence that you will be loved and valued regardless. As I said above, this openness doesn't necessarily require work or effort. On the contrary, it requires that we give up the effort required to stay closed and maintain a false front. The mistake many make, however, is to focus too much on the practice of openness, thus trying too hard to be open. This often makes the openness seem contrived and the intimacy artificial. The better approach is to focus on creating a secure environment where openness and intimacy won't have to be forced. When people feel secure they are naturally inclined to open their hearts and spirit. When both partners relax and allow themselves to be who they are with no unnatural barriers erected, they will have created security, and intimacy will simply happen. Security sets a soothing tone that will allow you to feel relaxed in your marriage. That underlying uneasiness that may have previously destroyed intimacy just quietly fades away.

Another major factor in creating security is commitment. Two of my favorite marriage experts, Dr. Scott Stanley and Dr. Howard Markman, tell mates to think of commitment as having two components: (1) a plan to stay connected until death, and (2) a list of reasons why they can never live in disharmony or get divorced. Just think how safe you would feel if the two of you had a mutual plan for living together the rest of your life. Well, I will provide that plan at the end of this book by showing you how to create a marriage constitution. In addition, you can make for yourself a huge list of all the reasons why you can't divorce—the kids will suffer, your parents will be disappointed, God will not be pleased, it costs too much, the pain of separation is too great, holidays will be sad and complicated, child custody fights, court fees, and on and on, until the list is exhausting. Thinking about your life-time commitment to each other really works to build security.

The Garden of Eden was a supremely secure place. Adam and Eve felt no fear there. Before they sinned, they enjoyed an amazingly intimate relationship with God and each other. The couple felt so close to one another that God described them as "united into one."[2] Nothing came between Adam and Eve— not insecurities, not sharp differences of opinion, not even clothes! They were completely open with each other. No walls, no masks, no fear. Their marriage blossomed.

The foundational component of an excellent marriage is a truly secure environment—one that is secure physically, intellectually, spiritually, and emotionally.

When you have a state-of-the-art security system built into a marriage it makes opening up significantly easier. When both of you are committed to creating a secure marriage, you avoid things that would cause hurt in each other, and you begin building a foundation for a great relationship. Ideally, your home should feel like the most secure place on earth.

Security and the Bamboo Tree

I sometimes liken security in marriage to something I discovered in the story of the Chinese bamboo tree. What's so special about this tree? The bamboo tree does not produce much noticeable outward growth for the first four years of its life. Even when it enjoys the right kind of soil, water, sunlight, and weeding, observers see nothing on the surface except a little bulb and a small shoot. That doesn't sound like the perfect marriage relationship, you say? Read on.

The Chinese bamboo tree may look like it's not developing as it should, but remarkable things are happening underground. The tree is busy putting out thick and long-ranging roots called rhizomes. The plant limits its surface growth while its network of roots reaches deep and wide, providing a firm base for massive growth. If you looked at a young Chinese bamboo tree in its fourth year, you might think, *that is the puniest, most pathetic tree I've ever seen. It's been sitting there several years without any noticeable growth. There must be something wrong with it.* So you decide to pull it up. You take hold of that tiny tree and pull with all your might. Nothing happens. So you yank, and jerk, and twist, and tug, but the tree doesn't budge. No matter how much sweat and energy you put into it, you cannot pull that Chinese bamboo tree out of the ground.

Then in the fifth year of growth, the Chinese bamboo tree shoots up to a staggering height of eighty feet. Can you imagine? Something that had been growing without much visible progress for four years in the next year alone develops into an eighty-foot tree!

The same thing can happen in your marriage when you focus on security. Build security as the foundation of your marriage, and nothing can pull it apart. Security is the root system of a flourishing marriage. The growth may not be immediately visible. Disagreements, misunderstandings, and setbacks will occur. But if you keep yourselves open to each other, communicating and listening from the heart, your lives will grow and intertwine beneath the surface, solid and secure. Build the root system of security as the basis for your marriage and watch it soar to new heights.

Security in a Promise

Think of a group of typical boys, mostly ten or eleven years old, playing together after school in the woods. They pretend they are explorers lost in a dense, tropical jungle, facing lions, tigers, snakes, and other man-eating creatures. Poor little Jeff is a couple of years younger than the rest. Being much smaller, he can't run as fast through the underbrush. Occasionally the older boys forget Jeff is there, and run on ahead of him. On one occasion they run so far ahead that he feels lost, isolated, and scared. When they come back to him, he doesn't want to play anymore and insists that the others take him home. Well, none of them wants to go home until dinnertime, and none wants to waste valuable daylight escorting this kid back, especially when they know his early return will prompt questions from parents, and they'll all be in big trouble for neglecting the poor kid. So they tell Jeff that they will not run away from him again. But he is not convinced. Maybe he has good reason to doubt that they will do what they say.

So he asks, "Do you promise?"

"Yes," they answer. "We promise. We will never run off and leave you again." With that Jeff is satisfied, and the boys continue their game.

Even to kids playing together, a promise means something that a mere declaration does not. Simply saying what you intend to do is not enough. You might have your fingers crossed, or you might come back later and say, "I was just kidding."

The same was true when I was a kid. A promise was a solemn bond, and we boys all knew it. If we backed up any declaration with "I promise," you could take it to the bank. "I promise" meant you were committed to do what you said you would do. It gave the other party security, because he could depend on follow-through on the thing promised. Of course, you can say that the words "I promise" should never have been necessary. We should have had enough integrity to do what we said we would do without having to buttress the validity of our word with the assuring phrase. True enough, but we were kids, and to us it sometimes took the extra emphasis of those two words to give us the security we were looking for.

I've long since grown up, but one thing I haven't outgrown is the sense of security that comes with a promise. I have found this to be especially true in my marriage. When I promise something to my wife, Norma, or when she promises something to me, we both know that we can depend on that thing happening. A promise means no excuses. It means I will climb volcanic mountains and swim shark-infested waters, making every possible effort to fulfill my word regardless of obstacles, unforeseen difficulties, circumstances, or my emotional climate.

Come to think if it, that's the kind of promise you made when you launched your marriage. It was built into your wedding vows. You promised to love and cherish your mate "for better or for worse, in sickness and in health, till death do us part." That was your first married promise, and it was not conditional. It had no term limits or expiration date. It was meant to remain in effect from that moment until one or both of you leave this earth for the kingdom of heaven. That promise was meant to provide a solid base of security for your marriage. Whatever happens, you have promised to love your husband or your wife. It doesn't matter whether you get upset with each other. It doesn't matter if you get bored with the routine. It doesn't matter if the money you expected is not there. It doesn't matter if either of you loses your attractiveness, turns grumpy, sour, or uncommunicative, gets a debilitating illness, or falls into deep depression. You will love him. You will cherish her. You promised. And that promise gives your marriage security.

I know a man who, when his wife asked why he loved her, would answer, "Because I promised I would." Well, that may not be exactly the answer she was looking for. No doubt she was fishing for something a little more romantic, like, "Because you are beautiful, wonderful, intelligent, sexy, lovely, desirable, and practically perfect in every way." (Eventually he "got it," by the way, and now responds with an answer that conveys a little more of a romantic feeling.) Yet his wife was not altogether put off by his first answer. Why? Because it gave her a sense of security. His love was not based on her performance, her attractiveness, or any condition she had to meet. She did not have to worry about living up to some standard to earn it. His love was based on his own integrity. He had promised to love her, and by gum, he was determined to do it. Romantic? No. But reassuring? Very! I'll let you in on a great secret: the more secure mates feel with each other's love, the more their feelings of affection toward one another will grow.

Perhaps this man still needed to learn that out of that first, overarching promise, other promises needed to grow. The tree had been planted, but the root system needed to expand and take hold. Or to use another metaphor, the promise to love "for better or for worse, in sickness and in health, till death do us part" sets a wonderful foundation for a secure marriage, but the house still needs to be constructed upon it. And that means other promises need to be made in order to build security into the marriage from the ground up. A secure house needs more than just a solid foundation; it needs impenetrable walls, strong doors, dependable locks, a protective roof, and a working security system. A secure marriage needs more than just that initial, undergirding, "forever" promise; it needs a series of subsequent promises to build safety into every facet of a couple living together and developing greater intimacy.

In Scotland, about twenty miles southeast of Edinburgh, stands a small but beautiful castle built in 1430 by a nobleman named Lord Borthwick. The back side of the keep (the main tower, or living quarters) of Borthwick Castle bears a huge scar high in the wall where missing and broken stones create an indention perhaps three feet deep. The cause of the damage was cannon fire in the mid-seventeenth century when Oliver Cromwell attacked, intent on punishing the Borthwick residents for having harbored Catholics during his Puritan sweep of Britain. Many castles would have been breached or would have collapsed after a three-foot penetration of their walls. But not Borthwick. Its walls range from ten to twelve feet thick. No doubt Cromwell could have eventually breached the castle with continuing cannon fire, but he chose to stop the bombardment and let its inhabitants go free leaving the castle to them, rather than expend the time and ammunition it would take to bring it down. In fact, Borthwick's walls are so strong that in World War II when all Britain was under threat of German air attack, Scotland's most precious records were moved out of government offices in Edinburgh and stored in Borthwick Castle.

Don't you long for a marriage that is secure? A place of utter safety with strong walls of love surrounding and protecting you and your mate, instead of walls of deception standing between you. A place where you can relax and be yourself, unafraid to open your heart, unafraid that your love will suffer the ravages that are tearing marriages apart all around you. In this book I want to do one thing for you and for other couples reeling from all the attacks bombarding marriages today from without and within. I want to show you how to build your marriage on a solid foundation of security that will protect both of you and enable your marriage to grow into the kind of blissful intimacy you have always dreamed of having. I want to show you the promises you can make to your mate that will enable him or her to feel like there is a ten-foot-thick secure wall around both of you strong enough to make you want to open up the innermost recesses of the heart. Remember: *when couples feel secure with each other, each is naturally inclined to open his or her heart to the other.* As a result, intimacy just happens. It does not require effort or conscious attention. Therefore, the only way to enjoy a close, open, intimate marriage is to create a safe environment.

Every chapter and every promise in this book is designed to promote security, so that you can have a marriage filled with deep love and intimacy. Each is designed to lessen the risks involved in achieving intimacy and enable you to connect without getting hurt. When you read and apply these promises, you will discover the way to create a secure place in your marriage.

Coming Up Next...

If security is the lock that protects every marriage, what is the key to that lock? There is one thing that couples can do for each other that will keep security intact. That's what we'll explore in the next chapter.

CHAPTER 2

The Power of Honor

Lee's Asian family would not accept his wife, Angie, because she was White. Not only was she White; her Caucasian features were extreme, including blonde hair, blue eyes, and fair skin. The women in Lee's family hated Angie. At family gatherings his eight siblings—especially his sisters—would hound her, harass her, pick fights, and do whatever they could to show that she was not accepted into the family. They criticized and even slandered her in an attempt to make her look bad in the eyes of Lee, hoping to break the couple apart. As you can imagine, at family gatherings Angie's life was miserable.

Angie clearly remembers the day it all changed. She remembers the incident that not only stopped the abuse, but also became the defining moment in her marriage. Here's how she described it:

"Lee and I had been at the home of his family in Sacramento for a few days of vacation. As usual, I had been verbally abused and insulted from the moment we walked in the door. But our stay was finally over, and the two of us had just left the house and gotten into our SUV to head home. At that moment Lee's sister Kim, who was always the most rude to me, came up to Lee's window and began yelling at him, 'I can't believe you're sticking with this White @#*%!'

"Lee shifted the gear to park and looked steadily at his angry sister. 'Kim,' he said. 'Angie is my wife. I love her dearly. I will never leave her, and I will never let anything come between us. If you force me to choose between her and this family, I choose her.'

"Kim glared with contempt and opened her mouth to speak again, but Lee stopped her and repeated the words he had just spoken, softly but as firmly as the Rock of Gibraltar. Kim said nothing. She looked from him to me for a moment, then simply said, 'Okay' and walked away.

"Words fail me to tell you how Lee's words made me feel. They sent a thrill through my whole being almost like an electrical charge. I had never felt more loved, more honored, more secure."

And there's more to Angie's story. Because of the way Lee honored his wife, the attitude of his whole family changed. From that moment on, she suffered no more abuse from them. Soon they accepted her, and not long after this incident it became clear that they even loved her as one of the family.

When Angie and Lee went back to Sacramento, that defining moment in their marriage was brought up before the entire family. Kim explained her own feelings, which accurately reflected those of the rest of the family. "Remember that day when Lee told me for the first time that he actually loved you? Because of the way he honored you, at that moment I knew I had to change."

From that day forward, Angie became closer to Kim than to her own biological sister. Lee's honor of her established her worth and value at such a high place in his heart that his family could not help but see her in the same light. And in the process of honoring her, he created security for her. She knew he valued her higher than any other earthly relationship, and he would let nothing come between them. He put an effective home security system around Angie—one that protected her from all possible security breaches.

The Gift of Honor

During the early years of our marriage, I had no idea what it meant to honor a wife. It didn't occur to me that considering her interests and taking seriously her needs that differed from my own were ways of honoring her. But her pet cat, Puff, taught me a valuable lesson. I didn't like that cat. I didn't want it in the house, and I was constantly trying to keep it out. I didn't like all the cat hair or the scratched furniture. I yelled at the kids if they tried to bring Puff into the house. I had

groups of people in for Bible studies, and I imagined that
some might be allergic to cats. I had more honor for my
ministry than I did for my wife and children.

Then one day I accidentally ran over Puff while backing
out of the driveway. (Yes, it really was an accident.) Chaos
broke out in my home—wailing, tears, recriminations, and
grief. And much of the grief was mine—not over the cat, but
because the surprising intensity of my family's pain showed me
how I had failed to honor them by devaluing something that
they valued highly. I remember the turnaround in my attitude.
As I listened to the pain of each of my kids, I was gentle and
caring in my comfort. Afterward I went into the bedroom,
knelt down next to the bed and took Norma's hand. I humbly
and sincerely told her how sorry I was about Puff, and after a
while she looked toward me and said,

"I know you didn't mean to murder Puff."

I could have corrected her by saying that at the most it was
manslaughter, but I merely held her hand and sought her
forgiveness for all of the mean things I had said about poor little
Puff. That day I understood how much an animal meant to my
family, and how it was an act of dishonor to them not to affirm
the animal's value. We've had some type of animal ever since.
From this family struggle, the concept of honor began to dawn
on me.

Now honor in marriage has been the cornerstone of my
writing and speaking for over forty years. And the reason is
that honor is so basic to security in marriage. When one mate
shows high honor to the other, the recipient of that honor

feels secure in the marriage and responds accordingly by reciprocating in many positive ways, which I will discuss in this chapter. And honor is so simple. Honor basically means to value another person highly—to see him or her as extremely important and of great worth. If you want that in the form of a definition, the one I prefer is "to give preference to others by attaching high value to them." A person who is highly honored will be thought of as a cherished treasure and treated with the kind of respect we give to royalty.

In his research, relationship expert, Dr. John Gottman, found honor to be such a bedrock to a satisfying relationship that he can now predict divorce with nearly 100 percent accuracy just by observing whether mates honor each other. In my own studies and observation of couples, I've found that honor isn't merely important to marriage; it is absolutely critical. Without honor, you cannot attain intimacy or security in a relationship. In fact, it's impossible to create even a functional relationship without honor. Dr. Scott Stanley of Denver University told me that without honor between a married couple, no amount of relational skills will work to keep them closely connected in love. Honor has got to be the center of the marriage. Scott told me that if marriage were a car, honor would be the gasoline.

"What?" I can hear some readers say, "You want me to honor *him*—that creep who plays golf all day Saturday, watches sports all day Sunday, ignores me in the evening, and at night snores like a buzz saw?" Or "You expect me to put *her* on an honor pedestal? She spends half her life watching soap operas with cream all over her face, contradicts every decision I make, and nags me for not taking out the trash. Why should I honor her?"

Well, of course, if you choose to look only at your mate's shortcomings, he or she may not seem to deserve honor. But that has nothing to do with it. Honor is not earned; it's a gift. It isn't purchased by your mate's actions or contingent on your own emotions. You give honor because you choose to give it, whether or not it's deserved or even wanted. It's a decision you make. You just do it. Remember, when you said your wedding vows you promised to love. As we noted in the previous chapter, that promise was unconditional, "for better or worse," which means not dependent on health, happiness, prosperity, or the deserving character of your mate. To honor is like your decision to love. It is a decision you make. It's not a matter of your mate's deserving, but of your own integrity. Your affectionate feelings will flow from how much honor you give your mate, not from how easy or hard they are to live with.

Your Honor Can Reflect
God's Value for Your Mate

Honor is a way of accurately seeing the immense value of a person made in God's image. God created each one of us as a one-of-a-kind person with unique gifts and a unique personality. God sees each of us as precious and valuable because He sees the innate worth that He built into us.

When God brought to Adam the newly created Eve in

all her naked glory, can you imagine what he thought? *Wow! When God said He'd give me a companion, never in my wildest dreams did I imagine anything like this. Man, what a treasure!* Can you imagine the tingling thrill Adam must have felt the moment he first touched her?

Now, think back. Didn't you feel the same way when you married your mate? Didn't it feel as if you had discovered a cave filled with priceless gold, silver, diamonds, and sparkling gemstones? And it was true. When you married, you received a treasure of unfathomable worth. You will never be able to understand all the wonders God has given you in your marriage partner. Just the physical differences alone are unimaginable. The cells, organs, hormones, features, and shape all combine into a magnificent being who has value above the angels. As the Scriptures say, we are a marvelous creation, a spectacular wonder with splendor above the worth of all creation. Adam was right to gape in wonder when he first saw Eve. You were right to gape in wonder when you married your mate. And maintaining that wonder is critically important, because it means you are still finding reasons to honor your spouse.

Picture your mate as personally autographed by God. Wouldn't you feel thrilled to be seen with someone who bore God's personal autograph? Wouldn't you want to have your picture taken with such a person and hang that picture in a prominent place on your wall? Once you start thinking like God and realize the supreme value of that other person in your life, your treatment of your mate should communicate to them that you are bending your knee in the presence of a highly honored person, or giving a standing ovation to a soloist after an outstanding concert. When you look for the good and the honorable in your mate, you will find it because it is there. God instilled His glory into each one of us.

Adam and Eve's value was enormous. They were, after all, handcrafted by God Himself and He loved them dearly. But when this couple chose to disobey God, they showed by their actions the age-old, basic sin of all mankind from that time forward: *God, we don't trust Your ways any more; we'll go our way and You go Yours.* By taking this action they tarnished the glory that God had built into them in the same way that rust ruins the glistening sheen of steel. C. S. Lewis reminds us, however, that the original glory is still there, lying just beneath the surface of every human, waiting for the day it will again be brought into the open. He said that in all our everyday dealings with each other, we must "remember that the dullest and most uninteresting person you can talk to may one day be a creature which, if you saw it now, you would be strongly tempted to worship. . . . There are no ordinary people." [1] When we look at each other, it's all too easy to see only the rust on the surface—the irritating habits, the failures, the broken promises—and forget that beneath the tarnish the pure steel is still intact. All the glory that God created in us is still there, waiting for the moment when that coating of sin is scoured away. As we are transformed more and more into His image, we actually start looking more and more like Him, reflecting His loving nature.

You can learn to see this inner, godlike glory that God's own hand infused into your mate. It may not be easily visible at first, but when we look past the failures and weaknesses and affirm the immense value God created into every one of us, we see that honoring each other is appropriate. When I choose to look at the inner value of my wife, I'm simply looking at her as God looks at me. And I'm so very glad He sees me as He does. I would cringe to think that my Creator sees only my weaknesses and judges me by my stumblings and bumblings. Instead, He sees my potential, my innate worth, complete with all the godlikeness that He instilled into me originally. Honor is so simple, really. All we need to do is look at each other as God looks at us. When you develop that kind of honor for your mate, you help create a secure environment in which great relationships can flourish.

The apostle Paul encouraged the early Christians to build their relationships on this kind of honor when he wrote, "Be devoted to one another in brotherly love; give preference to one another in honor" (Romans 12:10 NASB).

Feelings Follow Beliefs

Why is it so important that you honor your loved one as a costly gift or special treasure? Because, as my friend, clinical psychologist Dr. David Stoop says, our thoughts create our emotions. In his book, *You Are What You Think*, he quotes the Greek philosopher Epictetus as saying, "Men are disturbed not by things, but by the view they take of them." Stoop goes on to amplify what Epictetus meant: "He understood that in every situation, our responses are based on how we choose to interpret that event. And that choice creates our emotions."[2] In other words, it's not what happens or exists that affects us; it's how we *look at and respond* to what happens or exists. We have various ways of saying this: "You can see the glass as half empty or half full." "You're as young as you think you are." "You can do it if you think you can." Or as the Bible tells us, "As a man thinks in his heart, so he is." And in the words of Jesus Himself, "Where your treasure is, there your heart will be also" (Matthew 6:21 NASB). You decide what is valuable to you, and your emotions will fall in line and validate that choice. I watched my own beliefs and feelings toward Norma change as I found the Bible verses that speak to her value as God sees her. As I memorized those verses and let them sink into my heart, my affectionate feelings toward her increased.

You can make the choice to look beneath the surface behavior of your mate and find the value inside. You decide in your heart, on your own, that you will treasure her; that you will honor him as valuable. You will look at all the plusses instead of the minuses. And it will work. Your emotions will fall in line and validate your choice because it is our nature to place our affections, desires, and enthusiasm on whatever we treasure highly. Our feelings always follow our beliefs and thoughts. Make the decision to treat your mate as a 100-carat diamond, and your positive feelings for him or her will increase.

This is called "confirmation bias." Confirmation bias

means that regardless of what we believe about someone, whether positive or negative, we will find evidence to support that belief. This can have a major impact on your relationship with your loved one. If you do not see your mate as a priceless treasure, then you will tend to focus on his or her negative actions as evidence of low worth. And it's inevitable; you will treat your mate accordingly. On the other hand, if you choose to look at the positive side and see your mate as a wonderful treasure, then you will focus more on his positive behavior as evidence of high worth. Both the positive and the negative are always there. Which you focus on is simply a matter of your choice.

Choosing to notice your mate's positive behavior is essentially what we are told to do in Scripture. As the apostle Paul said, "Finally, brethren, whatever is true, whatever is honorable, whatever is right, whatever is pure, whatever is lovely, whatever is of good repute, if there is any excellence and if anything worthy of praise, let your *mind dwell* on these things" (Philippians 4:8 NASB). Think of the good qualities of your mate and you will begin to place a high value on one another. And the happy surprise is that your feelings of affection will grow by leaps and bounds. When this happens, honor flows easily.

Honor Is Action

Our beliefs generate our thoughts, and our thoughts create our emotions, but the chain doesn't end there. Our emotions go on to motivate our behavior. Not only must you pledge to honor your mate by thinking positively of him in your mind, but you must also convey honor through your words and actions.

There's a story about a husband who was known to be a man of few words. His wife longed for a little romantic conversation, but it never came. One evening when he was engrossed in his newspaper, she asked, "Steve, do you still love me?" He replied, "I said I did when we married, didn't I? If anything ever changes, I'll let you know."

Steve may have done all the right things I outlined above. He may have chosen to focus on his wife's good qualities. He may have cherished her as a pearl of untold value. He may even have felt that all this meant he was honoring her. But clearly honor wasn't getting across to her as long as he kept his feelings bottled up inside. Honor is not really honor until it is expressed and demonstrated. Those positive emotions for your mate that you hold in your heart must somehow find their way out through your mouth. You'll find it much easier and more natural to speak the honor you feel for your mate after you've read chapter four.

It's a fine thing to verbalize the honor you feel for your mate, but those thoughts take on even more meaning when they are expressed in action. You must show your honor not only in what you say, but also in what you do. I'm reminded of a letter that one young man wrote to his girlfriend who lived across town back in the days before automobiles were common. "I would climb the highest mountain for you," he gushed. "I would swim the deepest river just to be where you are. I would fight alligators, lions, and tigers to be by your side. I would walk through fire just for the privilege of gazing into your eyes. And I'll see you Saturday night if it doesn't rain." The wimpiness of this young man's intention yanked the rug out from under his high-sounding words, and all the honor they expressed tumbled into meaningless rubble. The honor you give your mate is not just in what you choose to think. It's not even in what you feel about her. You show honor in how you speak to him or treat her. I'll give you a few concrete hints on how to do this in a moment.

Honor Makes People Honorable

There's a principle in quantum mechanics that says the act of observing the particles inside the structure of an atom actually affects their behavior. I know nothing about quantum physics, but I do know that a similar principle applies to honor. Not only does showing honor cause your feelings toward your mate to change, as we discussed above, but it also affects behavior. You will find that your partner will respond to the honor you show by trying to live up to it.

I love the story about a group of seventeen-year-old senior high school boys who devised a class project that involved picking a homely girl and systematically seeking dates with her and documenting the result. The project was potentially cruel and risky, but the boys were desperate for better grades. They chose as their subject (or victim) a fifteen-year-old sopho-more girl who was afflicted with many of the common problems that often result from teenage growth—facial blem-ishes, awkward bearing, ill-fitting clothing, and insecure shyness. The boys dated this girl, one after the other. Each of them memorized a preprinted list of compliments, which they used to extol her beauty and desirability. These boys often met after class to laugh about how the girl was happily as-tounded at her newfound social life, but had no idea that it was all a hoax.

But an unexpected thing happened. After several weeks of this, the girl began to wear more attractive clothing and learned better use of her makeup to enhance her features. She gained confidence in herself and became more outgoing and friendly. Soon she was one of the most popular girls on campus. Not only were other boys eager to date her, but those involved in the experiment actually began to compete in earnest for her affection. But to their great disappointment, she settled on the most sought-after boy in school—one who had not been part of the experiment.

This story shows that what others think of us, and esp-ecially the way they treat us, has a profound effect on the deep-seated beliefs we develop about ourselves. The senior boys treated this girl as a treasure, and as a result she became a treasure. She responded to the honor she was given—artificial though it was—by becoming a person worthy of honor.

It almost always works. We tend to live up to what people think we are. When your wife comes into the room wearing a new dress (or not wearing one!) and sees your jaw drop in amazement, your eyes light up with fascination and childlike wonder, then she can begin believing that maybe she is everything your actions indicate her to be. She can believe that she is worthy of the honor you give her, and that fact gives her great security. Honoring your mate is a surefire way to improve your marriage.

How Do I Put Honor into My Marriage?

It's likely that when most of us think of honoring someone, the first thing that comes to mind is something like a company dinner given to recognize a departing employee. Or maybe it's a ceremony, like those we see on TV when the President makes a short speech and places the Medal of Honor on the neck of a war hero. Well, it might not be such a bad idea for you to have a ceremony to honor your husband for faithfully taking out the trash every Thursday, or your wife for getting the kids off to school every morning. But that kind of ceremony is not really what I'm talking about. In a nutshell, you honor your wife by treating her as if she were the most valuable creature on the planet. You honor your husband by treating him as if you were the luckiest woman in the world for snaring him. In action, this means you are attentive to her needs or sensitive to his moods. It means that you continually put your mate first and seek the best for him in all situations. Here are a few practical suggestions for showing honor.

Honor is becoming a student of your mate. You honor your mate by being attentive to his or her preferences. But do you really know those preferences? What is your husband's favorite food? What is your wife's favorite kind of date? What does he love to do on vacation? What does she like to do to relax? What is his idea of having a good time? Sadly, many husbands and wives cannot answer even these simple questions about each other's tastes and preferences.

When my boys were young, I often bought them toys for Christmas or birthdays that had to be assembled. These always came with an instruction manual. But, hey, I didn't need that. I could see how the parts fit together just by looking at their shape. Yep. You guessed it. After a couple of hours of frustration and half a dozen leftover bolts, I grudgingly picked up the instruction manual and started over.

It's too bad that your mate didn't come with an instruction manual. How can you honor someone without knowing how all the parts work—the hot buttons, preferences, loves, hates, joys, favorite everythings, and pet peeves? Well, you need to create an instruction manual. I don't really mean you need to write out these things, but you need to know them. And you need to use that knowledge as a basis for personalizing the honor you give to your valued mate. Do the things he likes. Avoid the things that turn her off. Make the honor fit the person. Make your mate feel like the most valued person on the face of the earth.

Do sweat the small stuff. Husbands and wives sometimes make the mistake of thinking of honor as being only the big things they do for each other, like buying her a new car or giving him tickets to the Super Bowl. Those things are great, but the big, spectacular things don't make up for the little things you should be doing all the time. Guys, it's good to be attentive to the house. That's her nest, you know, and she knows you honor her and are concerned about her security when you repair a leaky faucet, re-glue a sheet of buckling wallpaper, replace a loose doorknob, or keep the lawn mowed. Girls, he loves it when you send out his clothes for cleaning, cook his favorite steak, or watch a ball game with him. And how about those old-fashioned courtly things, like opening the door for her or pulling out the chair at the restaurant? Little courteous attentions are not really so little. They are ongoing evidence that mates honor each other and desire to create security in their marriage.

Make yourself appear worthy. Your own personal appearance can reflect the high value you place on your mate. If you value him highly, you will want to make yourself a partner worthy of his value. If you are fifty pounds overweight and he looks like an NFL linebacker, you will honor him by starting to count calories and getting on the treadmill. If she's a sharp dresser with coordinated outfits and coiffed hair, it's time for you to get a haircut and throw away your holey jeans and faded T-shirts. After all, you don't want to be seen with a queen looking like a slob, do you?

I look at those macho guys on TV and in movies today and notice that most of them look as if they haven't shaved in three or four days. Girls must think that's cool. But when I try to look hunkish by letting my stubble grow, Norma's reaction is far from what I hope. She doesn't see the GQ look that I'm after; she thinks I look like I just walked in off the street to beg a handout. So I go and shave.

You honor your mate by taking care of yourself—your health, your grooming, your clothes, and your general appearance.

Honor is seeking forgiveness when you have wronged your mate. No matter how sincere our intent to honor, we all have lapses and failures. I had one recently. I was speaking in Hawaii, and early one morning I got up and went for a walk by the sea. I found a path that turned out to be extraordinarily beautiful, which led me through a magical pine forest. I lost myself in the beauty of it and forgot all about the time. When I finally returned to the hotel, there sat Norma in the lobby with that "you're in deep trouble, buster" glare in her eyes. I had forgotten that I told her to wait for me for breakfast.

"Where have you been for the last two hours?" she asked.

Two hours! Ohmygoodness! Was I gone that long? Maybe humor will disarm her. "I just took a little walk by the ocean for a couple of days—I mean minutes."

Bad idea. Not even the hint of a smile.

"What in the world happened?" she replied. "I was worried about you. I almost called out the helicopter patrol."

I understood instantly that Norma's hard-edged attitude was really an expression of her love. She was truly worried about my safety. After my heart attack, her imagination has worked overtime, and she had imagined all sorts of things that could have happened to me. Here sat this precious woman full of love and care for me, and I had been insensitive and callous to her feelings. How terrible! How stupid! Even now I wonder why I didn't take just a moment to call her on my cell phone. There was only one thing for me to do and that was to apologize with true sincerity.

"I am so sorry. I was wrong to forget the time or let even the beauty of nature to come between us. You are too important to me to be treated in such a way. What I did was not reflective of how much I adore you and see you as a special gift from God. You are the most important person on this earth to me. I feel as though I have wounded the Queen of England." After I asked her to forgive me, her heart melted.

A heartfelt apology without excuses has a powerful effect. When your mate knows that you value him enough to humble yourself and say you were wrong to do anything to offend, he feels honored.

List your mate's positive qualities. Earlier I talked about focusing on your mate's positive qualities instead of the negative. One way to spur yourself into honoring your husband or wife is to write these things down. Actually make a list of all the things you admire about her. Post these in a highly visible place in your home where you and, more importantly, your spouse can see them every day.

The great thing about a list instead of mental notes is that it somehow makes the good things about your mate seem more real. You've heard people say, "If it's in print, it must be true." Of course we know better; newspapers and books are not always trustworthy. Yet there's something to the idea of putting important concepts in writing. When you see it on paper, it's no longer just an abstraction; it has become a reality in the material world.

Everyone has great qualities worth committing to paper. Consider your mate's personality traits, appearance, thinking patterns, gender differences, faith, values, character, parenting skills, concerns, opinions, and life goals. Create the longest list you can by including every positive, precious, worthy, upbeat, godly, amazing, startling, and outstanding quality that you see. Personalize your list with real details you admire—not just her eyes, but her deep blue, expressive, mesmerizing eyes. Not just his care of the children, but his gentle and patient way of answering their many questions. Let your mate see your list and even exchange lists occasionally. That's honor. Then watch your marriage become more secure.

To give you a little extra motivation for making this list, one study found that over 70 percent of conflicted couples greatly improved their marriages by making just a two- or three-page list of positive qualities about their mates.

The Honor Journal

There is no better way to build the value of your mate than

to start writing a never-ending list of reasons why you believe your mate is valuable.

I have four and a half pages of qualities, actions, physical characteristics, attitudes, behaviors, character traits, memories, gifts received, and so on about why my wife is so incredibly important to me. I am a dreamer and she is the dream maker. Her creativity and attention to detail work to find ways of achieving the dreams God gives me. She has an incredible way of steering me with her heart. Recently we were reminiscing about some of the decisions I have made during our life together. In each of those decisions, her wisdom guided me. Her heart told me when to move forward, when not to move forward, when to plunge in, or avoid a situation altogether. Without her, my fondest dreams would never have materialized.

The longer your list of your mate's valuable traits, the greater will be your honor.

Make a promise to honor. Remember that one of the promises in your wedding vow was to honor. Maybe like Steve, you feel that you've already said it once, so there's no need to say it again. Not! In that sense, honor is just like love. Saying it once is not enough. Your mate needs to know that your promise to honor has not faded with time. Let your wife know now and then that your original vow is still good by consciously pledging to put honor at the heart of your marriage. You and your mate must commit not just once, but over and over that each of you will consider the other to be the most valuable person in your life, worthy of honor without reservation. You must treat each other as treasures, and that attitude should govern all your actions and words.

Ultimately the way to put honor into your marriage is just to do it. It's a decision you make. Just do it, and soon you will soon see how honoring your mate gives legs to the words "I love you." It puts that statement into action. That kind of honor creates security.

The Ultimate Effect of Honor

As I close this chapter I want to tell a story to remind you of a point that I covered earlier—the result you can expect when you give honor to your mate.

There was a Polynesian island tradition that when a man wanted a bride, he had to give in payment to her parents something that he believed to be of equal value to what she was worth. Most men would give a pig, chicken, parrot, or some similar small animal. For the most beautiful of all women, a man might even be willing to give one of his prized cows.

One woman in the village who had just reached marriageable age was considered to be a little more plain and ordinary than most. Yet every girl had a few suitors, and she was no exception. One of these young men offered her parents a rabbit, another a chicken, and another a goose. One suitor came along, however, and offered the girl's father ten of his finest cows. Everyone was stunned. Such a bride price was unheard of. All the other young men walked away in disgust.

No woman is worth that!

The new suitor was thought to be foolish and extravagant. But he knew what he was doing. Knowing the value her suitor had placed on her, this Polynesian plain Jane began to hold her head higher as she strolled through the villages. She, after all, was now the famous "ten-cow woman." She paid more attention to her speech, her dress, and her way of conducting herself. She became more confident and elegant. Her facial expressions became kind and gentle, her body movements graceful and elegant, her voice soft and caring. In short, she became what she believed her worth to be and developed into the most stunning, beautiful, and graceful woman on the entire string of islands.

Everyone marveled at the young woman's transformation, and all thought the lucky young man had received full value for his high bride price. And indeed he had. The young woman responded to his honor by living up to his estimation of her. She rose to be worthy of the honor he bestowed upon her. He now felt like he was living with the queen.

This is a very important secret. If you place a high enough value upon someone, that person will usually move to justify that value. The same thing can happen in your marriage when you treat your mate with honor. It's the number one way to build the security you need for a growing and lasting relationship.

Coming Up Next...

What you are about to read in the next chapter will not only increase security for you and your mate, but if your experience is like mine, it will bring more enrichment and positive change to your marriage than anything you have ever done.

CHAPTER 3

The Truth about Change

Welcome or not, change is unavoidable. Life itself is change. Each moment is different from every other. Nothing remains static for an instant, from the planetary to the molecular level. Few of the changes we experience ourselves are under our control, whether it's the devastation of personal tragedy or simply unexpected rain.

But we can exert some power over the course of our own life. We can work to improve our economic situation, our family ties, and the condition of our homes. Some changes we can make entirely by ourselves—changes to our behaviors, thoughts, and feelings. And these are the kinds of changes I will address in this chapter—especially those that can strengthen your marriage and make it safer and more secure. Yet, these personal changes are also the most difficult, especially in a marriage relationship. They are difficult largely because we often approach them in the wrong way. Consider the case of Danny and Gwyn.

Gwyn wonders what in the world has happened to Danny since they married. In the first few weeks, he seemed to do everything right. He knew she loved a clean house, and he did his share of keeping things straight and tidy. And when he said he would do something, like carry out the trash, he would do it. But not anymore. He no longer follows through on his promises, and he doesn't even notice when things are dirty and cluttered. He just comes home from work, grabs the TV remote, plops down, and fails to follow through on the little responsibilities of keeping things straight, which should be normal behavior for any husband in America.

Friday they were expecting friends for dinner, and it was already Tuesday. Danny promised to clean out the garage, but he hadn't even touched it. Gwyn was getting more and more irritated. She had considered cleaning it herself, but certain parts of the house were his areas, and that included the garage. She's not going to clean it because once she does, he'll expect her to do it the next time and she'll never get his help on anything.

Danny came home from work whistling and happy. Holding up a rented DVD, he grinned and said, "Surprise! Look what I have! And popcorn, too. You'll love this movie. It'll make us want to cuddle all night long!"

Her eyes glared and her face scowled as she backed away from his attempt to embracc. "I can't believe you!" she cried. "How do you expect to clean the garage tonight and watch that movie at the same time? You let that garage get in such a mess it will take two days to clean it, and our company is coming in three! Did you totally forget this?"

Utterly taken aback, Danny throws the DVD across the room, pitches the popcorn toward the kitchen, and stalks out of the room. Tears of anger and frustration well up in Gwyn's eyes. *He's not the man I married,* she thinks, *and to tell the truth, I'm sometimes not really sure that I love him anymore.*

I'll tell you the rest of Gwyn and Danny's story later. But for now I want to point out that their problem is based on a huge misunderstanding of the truth about change. Without accurate information and guidance, you can believe something that's just not true and make a serious mistake about what is really going on in your marriage. You can believe you are falling out of love with your mate, when in fact your marriage is going through a normal transitional period. And you can have unrealistic expectations about what you can and cannot do to change your mate's behavior.

Thanks to our own marriage research center, we now have a high degree of certainty about what makes marriages work and what keeps them from working. We know that love doesn't last; you have to *make* it last. You must create a secure and safe environment that enables you to attend to the changes that occur in every marriage. If partners don't feel emotionally safe with one another, the instability these changes bring may jeopardize the marriage.

Misconceptions about Love

Most of us come into adulthood with a distorted vision of a

healthy love relationship. Our models of love often come from songs, books, friends, movies, and television, which depict love as fast blooming, overwhelming, intense, romantic, and requited. But these models display only one stage of love, the very first stage, which is heavily influenced by infatuation caused by chemistry. Good marriages contain many more elements than just chemistry, yet the lovers in these books and movies never get us far enough into the story to see them. We don't know whether the lovers stayed together long enough to determine if they were compatible or committed enough to stay the long term. We see an hour and a half of two people enduring misunderstanding and frustration, and then going romantically off into the sunset. We never get to see what happens next.

These images of love leave us with serious misconceptions, such as:

- Passion equals love.
- My lover should meet all my needs.
- Once love dies, you can't get it back.
- Chemistry is all that matters.
- Love conquers all.
- When things get tough, it means you have the wrong partner.
- My lover should make me happy.
- Once in love, you stay on a high forever.
- Love is a feeling, and you either have it or you don't.

These are all lies, or at best, gross misunderstandings of the true nature of love. The chemistry plays out. You eventually come off the high of infatuation. But that does not mean that love is dead. Not at all. In fact, it may be just beginning. It looks dead only because our expectations lead us to misunderstand the way love grows. It grows through four natural stages, and the better we understand these, the better we can adjust to the changes and keep love alive.

The Four Stages of Love

Dr. Pat Love, in her insightful book, *The Truth About Love*, identifies the four stages of love: infatuation, post-rapture, discovery, and connection.[1] The first stage, infatuation, is a magical time often considered to be the apex of life. It is characterized by focused attention on a specific person who gives you euphoric feelings and a new energy. You daydream about him or her when separated and can't wait until you are together again. You can see no wrong in your lover.

These feelings occur because your brain chemistry undergoes a drastic change. Your limbic system is flooded with a powerful chemical mix. It starts with the action of phenylethylamine (PEA), which is a naturally occurring neurotransmitter that acts like an amphetamine. Included in the love cocktail is dopamine and norepinephrine, which together with PEA trigger positive attitudes, increased energy, less need for sleep, loss of appetite, euphoria, excessive energy, no fear, and unrealistic optimism.

No wonder we say at this stage that love is blind, or that a person is "love-sick." No matter what fault our friends point out or what unsavory information is uncovered about the lover, the response is always, "We can work it out." Of course, this altered state makes us dangerously inclined to make decisions we may later regret. But after about six months, the euphoria begins to wane, and by the second year mother nature's love potion is mostly gone.

Stage two is what Pat Love calls the post-rapture stage. It's here that some people begin to think they are falling out of love. In neurological terms, the nerve endings in the brain have become habituated to the brain's natural stimulants. The brain develops a tolerance over a period of time, and when this happens, the body goes back to its normal state. It just can't continue the heightened level of physical and emotional activity. Psychologically, the novelty begins to wear off. Your behavior returns to your former self. Introverts talk less, pragmatists quit being spontaneous, angry people start losing their temper again, and so on. Anything from quiet acceptance to seriously questioning the relationship can characterize this stage.

If you married during the infatuation stage, the post-rapture stage can be particularly discouraging, and even dangerous to the marriage. Because marriage is so connected to our sense of security and safety, these descending feelings can create great anxiety. You can begin to think you married the wrong person. You might find yourself trying to command more time, attention, and information from your spouse. Or on the other extreme, you might withdraw into disappointed acceptance. Without the euphoria of the infatuation stage where you saw your mate through rose-colored glasses, his or her negative traits glare out at you. You may start focusing on what's wrong in the relationship rather than what's right. If a couple feels safe with each other, they will openly address these issues and be flexible enough to accommodate this change and learn new ways to love. And this will lead them into the next stage of change.

The third stage of love is the discovery stage. It's a time of learning about your own needs as well as those of your partner and redefining your way of loving to accommodate them. It's a time of gathering information about each other's deepest longings, beliefs, and fears. It's an opportunity to nurture your admiration and respect for each other as well as learning how to stay connected. It's a time to clarify roles and build trust. Stage three is also a time to learn how to solve your problems and create shared meaning by growing together in Christ. In short, this is a time to find out what really communicates "I love you" to your partner.

Dr. Love calls stage four the connection stage. It's characterized by expanding commitment, deepening connection, forging a friendship, and providing support. Living in a committed relationship gives you the opportunity to be truly known by another human being. I see this stage as the best time to increase the security and safety, because both mates feel freer to really open up the most sacred parts of their hearts. Intimate connection energizes you and takes you to heights beyond even the high of infatuation. When you connect with your partner, he becomes a primary source of your security. From their position of safety, supportive couples protect their marriage from outside forces by the way they think, act, and prioritize their life.

The Secret to a Secure Marriage

No matter what stage of love you are in—the delight of infatuation, the challenge of post-rapture, the excitement of discovery, or the blessings of connection—the key to dealing with the inevitable changes inherent in each of us is to focus on creating a secure environment for your relationship. All the behavioral skills in the world won't pump life back into an ailing marriage if the couple doesn't trust each other, if they don't feel safe, if they don't unconditionally love, if they don't feel valued and understood. In fact, some couples I've counseled used their newfound communication skills to fight more effectively. Now, I'm not saying marriage skills aren't helpful. I teach them regularly, even in this book, as you'll soon see. What I am saying is that unless couples feel emotionally safe, close, cherished, and respected, all the skill-building books and conferences in the world will fail to help them build the kind of marriage God wants for them.

And just what is the secret to building this kind of marriage?

Unconditional love. Love without criticism or expectation. It's the hardest kind of love to give, but the one that brings all the blessings you can hold. Would you like one good reason why you should love that blundering, frustrating, badly flawed spouse of yours unconditionally? It's simple: *we all need it.* When a baby is born, we love that child because he needs it. When people are starving, we feed them because they are hungry. When a friend is in emotional distress, we comfort her. And that's the reason Jesus expressed His unconditional love for us on the cross—because we needed it. He didn't require anything from us first. As He said, even "sinners" love the people who love them. The real test is how well we love someone who does not love us well. That is the true calling of Christ (Luke 6:32–33 NASB). A safe marriage is one in which each partner loves the other simply because the other needs it.

Shine the Spotlight on Yourself

After the marriage passes through the infatuation stage, many couples find loving each other unconditionally to be extremely difficult. No one marries a perfect partner. Negative traits and behaviors are difficult to live with. And without those euphoria-producing chemicals to help us see the magic in our mate, we begin to think the deflation of our feelings is due to some defect in him or her, a problem that we can solve by trying to change our mate's behavior. But that's not only a false belief, it's also unrealistic. God designed us to control ourselves, not each other. Using intimidation, aggressiveness, manipulation, guilt, or any number of other methods of persuasion seldom works. Sure, with enormous effort and persistence, it may be possible to change some things about another person. Some mates attack the other or play the victim so effectively that the partner feels bludgeoned or shamed into changing. But such a victory is hollow, because anything we get as a result of manipulation is far from unconditional love and is sure to be counterproductive in the long run.

Let's go back to Gwyn and Danny. The day after Gwyn's confrontation with Danny, she came to me, told me the whole story, and asked, "What can I do? I've tried to change Danny time and time again and nothing seems to work. Can you give me a really effective way for a wife to change her husband?"

"Gwyn, may I speak frankly to you?" I asked.

"Yes, absolutely," she replied.

"I know that you don't realize this, but the reason Danny irritates you is because you are guilty of the exact same thing that you are accusing him of. How about your own cleaning habits? How responsible are you about following through? You complain about Danny wasting time; do you spend your time productively? I have a tough time getting you on the phone because it either just rings because you're not there, or I get a continual busy signal. It seems like you are busying yourself with a lot of things."

My words hit home. Gwyn lowered her head and said, "You are so right. There are so many things that I should be doing around the house, but I do other things to avoid them, such as shopping with my girlfriends and staying on the phone constantly. I don't follow through on what I know I should be doing everyday."

"Now Gwyn, let me tell you something else," I said. "You may not want to hear this, but I don't have any great insight to help you change Danny, because it's impossible for you to do it. That's God's job. The changes Danny makes are between him and God. The same Holy Spirit is also in you, Gwyn, so what does that mean in terms of who you can change? It means that the only person you have the power to change is yourself. Let Him change you; let Him do the work that He needs to do in you. Let Him empower you to become more responsible in following through on your promises and forget about changing Danny. What you really need to do is to change so significantly that Danny sees the change and is then motivated to want to be more like you, which really means becoming more like Christ."

Gwyn, being a perceptive and humble person, got the point. In fact, she left me motivated and thrilled at her new insight. That evening she apologized to Danny with tears in her eyes: "I've been so wrong in trying to change you, trying to push you into becoming more responsible and cleaning out the garage. In fact, I want you to know that I am guiltier of this kind of behavior than you are. Honey, will you forgive me?"

That night they had a great time together, and the next morning he woke her up gently, saying, "Honey, I have a surprise for you." He led her downstairs and opened the door to the garage. It was sparkling clean. After she had gone to sleep the night before, he had gotten up and spent three hours cleaning up the mess. The humility of Gwyn's confession—admitting her own faults and promising not to ride him anymore—softened his heart and motivated him to change.

The Key to Lasting Change

This is the key to real, lasting love in your marriage: *change yourself* first and accept your mate unconditionally. Then as you work with God to become more like Him, watch how your mate will eventually try to emulate you. But don't do this just to change your mate; do it for yourself and for your own personal relationship with God. By taking responsibility for your actions and changing even small behaviors, you demonstrate unconditional love and thus create an emotionally secure atmosphere in which your marriage can thrive. Pushing your spouse to change in order to make you feel safer is hardly the way of unconditional love. When you want to change your mate, 99.99 percent of the time there's a selfish motive behind it. Expecting your partner to change to meet your expectations is putting self first. And if your mate does the same thing then you have two selves in conflict, each fighting to fulfill his or her own needs. The only way to improve the relationship is to shine the spotlight on yourself, and expose your own faults and weaknesses. Your mate may not want to deal with her problems, but you will be surprised at how great an impact your own example can have when you choose to deal with your own. You must not give in to feelings of hopelessness and helplessness, even if you are convinced that your partner is the real problem. Even if that is true, by changing yourself you can affect things dramatically and positively. I can hardly wait for you to reach chapter 6, because there I'll show you the easiest and fastest way possible to change anything about yourself.

Here's why you will influence change in your mate when you change yourself. As one person makes changes, those changes have a ripple effect on the other simply because your lives are connected and interact at many levels. Over time, you and your mate have shaped each other's behavior by consciously and unconsciously rewarding some behaviors and punishing others. Habits of behavior have been established. Patterns of relating are ingrained. In every marriage these patterns cause the relationship to achieve a certain kind of complementary balance. I don't mean it's necessarily a formal balance with equality of happiness and responsibility on both sides. One partner may be very aggressive and even over-bearing, while the other responds by becoming very passive and compliant. By balance I mean that each partner's attributes and responses adjust to accommodate each other. And they maintain some kind of equilibrium that way. Therefore, if one partner changes, the relationship changes, because the other automatically moves to adjust and maintain the balance.

So, when you take it upon yourself to change, you automatically change the balance of the marriage, and your mate must also change in order to maintain equilibrium. Even the slightest change is like adding a weight to one side of the balance. Your partner will sense the imbalance, feel un-comfortable, and adjust. I'll admit that now and then the partner's adjustment is for the worse, but not usually. When you make a truly positive change, it's highly likely that the corresponding change your partner makes will also be positive.

There are two kinds of changes you can make to improve a relationship: you can either increase pleasure, or decrease pain. To put it in behaviorist's terms, you can eliminate undesirable behaviors or increase desirable ones. The latter approach is not only more effective, it's also easier. It's much easier to do more of something a partner likes than to stop doing something he hates. And research indicates that this approach works better. Adding loving behaviors will reduce annoying ones.

Sometimes your mate may resist your new behavior. He or she might find even positive changes threatening simply because the balance has been upset. But if you persevere and remain consistent with your change, chances are excellent that your mate will eventually come around and change a certain behavior, too, and most often in a positive direction. This is what I call the *principle of reciprocity*. When you do even simple, random acts of kindness, such as back rubs, washing the dishes, giving flowers, or making a favorite dessert, your partner is likely to respond in a positive way. Your behavior influences your mate's behavior, and your mate's behavior rewards your behavior, making you want to reciprocate. It's not a vicious circle; it's a delicious circle.

Whose Fault Is It, Anyway?

My all-time favorite comic strip is the one from *Peanuts* where Charlie Brown attempts to kick a football held by Lucy. But she always jerks it away at the last minute, causing poor Charlie to fall flat on his back. Each year Lucy promises Charlie Brown that this time she will keep the football on the ground so he can kick it. Each year Charlie Brown is doubtful. He wavers. He remembers all the times that Lucy has yanked the football away. Each year Lucy gives Charlie plausible, sincere explanations why this time it will be different. And each year Charlie Brown believes her and races determinedly across the yard, where he falls with a thud when yet again Lucy yanks the football away.

If you are like me, you feel sorry for Charlie Brown. You also probably feel angry with Lucy. She's really being unkind. But has it ever occurred to you that Charlie Brown is being stupid? After all, he's been falling for the same old trick for years. When will he ever learn? What is he thinking? Well, obviously he thinks that this time, at long last, Lucy will not jerk the football away. And when she does, what does Charlie Brown do? He blames Lucy! Now think about this for a moment. Who's really at fault here?

I believe Charlie Brown is at fault. Here's why. Who, in the final analysis, is the cause of the problem? It's not Lucy. Lucy is not doing it to Charlie Brown. He is allowing this to happen to him. He hasn't learned a thing in all the years Lucy has been snatching the ball away. Unless Charlie Brown decides for himself to stop trying to kick the football, nothing will ever change. But if he changes *his* behavior and stops trying to kick the ball, two positive things happen: *he* avoids disappointment, and *Lucy's* behavior changes. She has no choice. She won't be able to take the football away.

Saying all this doesn't make Lucy right; it just means that Charlie Brown's happiness is always in his own hands. Happiness is always your choice, as we will see in a moment. When you feel unhappy or unfulfilled in your marriage, more than likely it means you have not done enough to create a secure environment where unconditional love can flourish. You need to focus your attention entirely on what you can do to become more loving—not on trying to change your partner—because that's what will make the greatest difference in your marriage and in your happiness. As long as we focus on being right and in control, insisting on the appearance of being correct while making our spouse appear to be wrong, the secure environment in which love can grow will elude us.

You probably don't want to hear this, but it's true. If you are unhappy in a relationship, you're the one who's probably at fault. A strong statement? Absolutely. But if you can come to grips with the truth of it, it will change your marriage and your life.

The Power of Choice

I said above that happiness is a choice. If I believe this I give myself enormous power. I won't wait for my wife to change and make me happy. I won't be trapped by blame, excuses, or self-pity. I'll be free to choose from the options available in any situation and respond in the wisest, most godly way I can. If something is wrong, my response won't be, "Someone's got to do something!" but rather "What does God want *me* to do?" If I believe that my happiness depends on what my mate does, I give up my free will and put my happiness in her hands. I may hate what my married life has become and blame my mate for betraying me by changing into something other than the sweet, loving person I married. I may think that if I complain or suffer enough, he will see the light and change and then feel obligated to rescue me from my unhappiness.

Don't buy this lie. Your mate is not going to rescue you. In my forty-plus years of marriage counseling, I've almost never seen this happen. One of the most common causes of pain and frustration is the fantasy that the mate will magically become a knight in shining armor to solve all problems and fulfill all dreams. It's not going to happen. You've got to take action yourself.

In physics, we learn the principle of inertia. An object moving in a particular direction will tend to continue moving in that direction unless something changes its course. Similarly, if you don't do something to change your life, your relationship with your partner will continue in the same direction. If you don't do something, *nothing is going to get better.* A classic definition of insanity is to keep on doing the same thing, but expecting different results. You are responsible for your own pain. You are the expert on your own needs, not your partner.

You are the one who must change your coping strategies to better meet those needs. How satisfied and happy you feel depends on the effectiveness of what you do for meeting your basic needs. If you want more intimacy, more pleasure, more cooperation in your relationship, you won't get any more than what you're presently getting, unless you change what you have been doing. It's up to you.

Taking responsibility to change yourself puts enormous power back in your hands. *You are now through with waiting and free to act.* To the degree that I empower my partner, imagining he will save me, I deplete my own power. In my failure to take responsibility for my own life, I condemn myself to passivity and helplessness. But if I believe that God's power dwells within me in the person of the Holy Spirit, I can with growing confidence make changes to redeem any situation in which I find myself.

Take a woman who believes that she can choose to be happy in her marriage. This is her belief. She's committed to being happy. If some difficult or tragic circumstance hits her, of course she will suffer for a time. This is normal. But check back with her later, and she will be happy again. She will have taken action to improve the situation. By contrast, take a woman who believes she's a victim of circumstances, that her husband is responsible for her happiness, that he must make up for her faults, that she has no control over her own well-being. Let things go wrong for her and she, too, will be unhappy. But check with her later, and even if her outward circumstances have improved somewhat, she will probably still be unhappy. Why? Because she will still be playing the blame game. She will feel out of control, and out-of-control people are basically unhappy people who in intimate relationships depend on the other person to meet their needs and make them happy. And it just doesn't work.

The Limits of Responsibility

So I'm asking you to first take responsibility for yourself. While your mate's behavior may be the cause of your dissatisfaction, and while it may even be that you have no corresponding fault of your own, your *response* is still up to you. And your response—not your mate's actions—is what determines your happiness. (I'll have more to say about this in chapter 4.) Nobody can change your marriage but you. You can't manage, motivate, or control your mate. Bottom line: you can't change your mate; you can only change yourself. To make your marriage work, you must first make yourself work. Once you recognize that you're completely responsible for your happiness, then you will be in a position to take charge of it and make it happen.

It used to really get to me when my wife corrected my driving. I told her time and again to cut it out, but to no avail. I used to believe that she did it just to ruin my day. It got to the point where I sulked and clammed up every time we rode anywhere. But now I realize the reason she felt the need to correct me. She almost died in a serious auto accident in high school and lost two of her good friends. When she thinks I'm veering too close to the edge of the road, she is simply reliving that terrible night. This caused me to change my thinking. I realized that she doesn't make me unhappy when she rags on my driving; I make myself unhappy with my prideful reaction to her criticism. I decided to understand the lingering trauma of her experience and have compassion and care for her. I admit that sometimes her criticism still gets under my skin a little, but now I use even this minor irritation as a spur toward growth. I have even started thanking her because God uses her comments to increase my patience and thus deepen my maturity with Him.

Someone has said, "Your freedom ends where my nose begins." That statement is simply recognition of the natural limits of responsibility. It's a recognition of the boundaries that separate one person from another, even people bonded in a marriage relationship. You have the freedom and responsibility to change yourself, but you have neither the freedom nor the responsibility to change another person, even your mate.

If you fail to grasp this principle and try to hold yourself responsible for changing your spouse, you will inevitably fail. Your failure may lead to anger, despair, hopelessness, or even guilt. I've seen both men and women torture themselves because, even though they have done their very best to change their mates, they have not managed to stop their negative behavior. "If only I knew the right thing to say or do," they lament, as if total power to change the other could be theirs if they just knew how to tap into it. They imagine that they should assume a power that no one possesses: the power to determine the choices of another human being. They might be good, orthodox Christians who believe in free will, but they act as if they don't accept the free will of their partner. They do not accept the boundaries that separate one human being from another. The truth is that both partners must assume appropriate responsibility for their own actions. Both must learn where self ends and the other begins.

Perhaps the worst thing about attempting to change your mate is that those attempts create an unsafe place for your marriage to thrive. And in time your mate will erect walls to ward off your continued push toward change. Trying to change your mate can only make your marriage worse and increase its chance of failure. If you've been pushing your mate to change, I urge you to stop it right now—today—and get on your knees and seek forgiveness for presuming to make the attempt. Promise that you are through browbeating your mate to change, and that from now on you're working in partnership with God to change only yourself.

I have discovered that we influence change in others far more powerfully when they can see how our own changes have worked for us. For example, I didn't think my wife was exercising enough to maintain her health, so for many years I badgered her to accompany me on my daily walks. She refused and began to react negatively because I brought it up so often. Finally I decided to quit bugging her about her exercise, but I kept on doing it myself. And guess what? You're right. Now she's up to six miles a day (mostly at the mall). I couldn't change her, but my own change motivated her to change.

The Precious Gift of Free Will

God has given you a *free will*. Next to the gift of His Son Jesus, this is the most precious gift you possess. It's what separates you from all other forms of life on this planet. Free will allows you to tap into strengths you never thought you had and exercise the power to change whatever needs changing in your life. Whatever grief or anger or pain you may feel about your marriage, you have the power within you to do something about it. You are not a victim. You are free to choose to act, to change. God has given you a huge reservoir of talent, creativity, knowledge, self-worth, energy, and love. You have the freedom to change your negative responses to your mate's behavior and draw on these God-given assets to do the right and helpful thing. Making this choice can introduce a redemptive force for positive change in your marriage.

I could summarize all I'm saying about change in this chapter by boiling it down to two critical things every married individual must exercise: unconditional love and personal responsibility. Unconditional love, as I mentioned earlier, means you accept and cherish your mate as he or she is. Personal responsibility means you take charge of correcting your own faults instead of your mate's. That, in a nutshell, is it. Intimacy, happiness, growth, communication and all the other vital aspects of a good marriage grow out of these two choices. If both partners recognize this fact, there will be no victims in the marriage. Each person's happiness will rest in their own hands. And the end result is the safety and security that every marriage must have in order to thrive.

Do you believe this? Really believe this? Since it's my contention that all behavior is a result of what we believe, this is a crucial question. Do you believe that you can take personal responsibility for the success of your marriage? If you don't, then you must believe the opposite—that your spouse or circumstances are in control of what happens to you. You must believe that you are a victim. Therefore you must react and put the blame on your mate when the marriage does not meet your expectations. This is a tragedy, because when you blame your mate you not only divest yourself of your responsibility, you also limit the choices you have to change the relationship. You forfeit the ability to control your own destiny.

The Choice of Making and Keeping Promises

So if you want your marriage to be the most exciting and rewarding journey of your life, the question to ask is not whether your mate is doing enough to make the marriage work. Rather ask yourself: "Am I loving my mate unconditionally by taking responsibility for my role in our relationship?" A good way to turn this intention into a commitment is to make a promise of it. Promise to look at yourself first, to take responsibility for your own part of the marriage and to stop trying to change your mate. Such a promise puts legs on unconditional love. It says you are willing to put your personal dreams and needs on hold for a while and make what's best for the relationship a priority.

For me personally, making promises is a very precious thing. The intimate connection Norma and I have as a result of our intentional commitment to each other is one of the unique experiences of life that I often find difficult to put into words. It enables us to revisit the glory when we first fell in love and then move on to the never-ending process of discovery, and back again, to an even deeper connection. Like good wine, love indeed gets better and better with time.

Coming Up Next...

I think the next chapter is my favorite. The principles I give you I've used in my own life to teach me how to quit being a victim. They have enabled me to take charge of my life—my feelings, my thoughts, and even my happiness and contentment.

PART TWO

The Five Promises that Create Security

CHAPTER 4

I Promise to Conform My Beliefs to God's Truths

All five of the promises in this book intertwine with each other, and each is crucial to building a great, loving, and secure marriage. But this promise is a favorite because of its life-changing effect on me. To explain what I mean, the following conflict with my wife used to be typical of many that occurred between us. But now such conflicts hardly ever happen. What made the difference? That's what I'm going to share with you in this chapter.

One Saturday morning I decided to do something loving for my wife. I decided to wash my own clothes in preparation for a trip. (Really now, isn't that about the most loving thing you ever heard of?) I wandered down to our laundry room and was about to throw my stuff into the washer when I noticed her lacey, white lingerie, along with a few sweaters and blouses, still in the washer. They had just finished washing.

I know the rule, place everything on the top of the dryer, and never ever attempt to dry her nice things. But I had a thought, and that was my undoing. *Maybe I could do an additional little something for her. I'll put these dainty things into the dryer for just five minutes.* I had seen her do this, taking them out while they were still wet and hanging them on these little circular clothespin hooks she has in the washroom. *That's a no brainer*, I thought. *Anyone can handle a job like this.* So I did.

I fully intended to come back in five minutes, but I got distracted. Two hours later I remembered and rushed downstairs. The lacey things were ripped and tangled, while the sweaters and blouses were all shrunk up to size twos. I was sick inside. My first thought was to put these things back into the washer and start the cycle again. No, that would be dishonest—but it was very tempting. Then I remembered that humor can defuse anger. So I came up with something I thought would be funny.

I approached Norma and announced that I had good news and bad news. Which did she want first? She gave me that "what have you done now?" stare. I had seen it many times.

"Which do you want," I repeated, "the good news or the bad?"

She asked for the bad news first. I apologized for what I was about to say and blurted, "I dried your clothes . . ."

She gasped and ran for the basement to assess the damage. But I caught her arm and said, "Wait, you haven't heard the good news. Our granddaughter, Taylor, has a whole new wardrobe." Norma never even cracked a smile. So much for humor. I suggested that we jump into the car and head for the outlet mall and replace everything.

"Don't you understand anything?" she snapped. "It will take hours to find each of these items. They don't all come from the same place."

"Oh really," I replied. I thought surely at a big department store we could find everything in about fifteen minutes.

At this point the meltdown began. I thought she was overreacting and making a big thing out of a minor incident. Furthermore, she didn't even seem to appreciate my good intentions in trying to help her. She accused me of wrecking her day, and in response I accused her of being too concerned about material things. Then she started lecturing me about things that had nothing to do with the current incident, like how I never remember anything. Now that really hurt. So I lashed back and accused her of caring more about her clothes than about me. That went over big. So big, in fact, that she turned and stalked out of the room. The next thing I heard was the door slamming and the car roaring out of the driveway and screeching down the street.

I was glad that she was gone. Here I made just a simple little mistake and she treated it like a seismic crisis. Where was forgiveness? If she really loved me as she should, she would have forgiven me. Now she had wrecked *my* day. Sure, I shouldn't have forgotten the dryer and ruined her things, but she should have considered my intentions and my feelings. I was angry and miserable for hours, and it was all her fault.

We inflicted this kind of misery on ourselves time and again until we began learning one of the greatest truths of our lives: *We* didn't make each other miserable; our *beliefs* made us miserable. What she did that day had nothing to do with my happiness or sadness. What I believed and how I responded had everything to do with it. This is not a new idea; Solomon said it a few millennia ago:

"For as he thinketh in his heart, so is he" (Proverbs 23:7 KJV)

What made me angry at that moment was the belief about her that I harbored in my heart. That belief was that Norma was a key source of my happiness, therefore my emotional equilibrium depended on her actions. So it's no wonder I thought Norma should be understanding and forgiving. Otherwise, I wouldn't be happy. When her actions did not meet the expectations of my belief, I was miserable. Had I not held the belief that she was the source of my happiness, what she did would not have had so much effect on my emotional equilibrium. My expectations were wrong because my beliefs were wrong. I had to learn that meeting my needs and expectations was not the reason God had placed her on earth.

It's not what others do to you or what circumstances you are facing or have faced that determine your moods, emotions, words, or actions. It's what you believe and think after these things happen to you that creates who you are.

As I studied this truth, I began to realize how often it is affirmed in the Bible. I found Scriptures such as these that told me without a doubt that the power of belief is no mere psychological concept, but is absolute truth.

- Above all else, guard your heart, for it affects everything you do (Proverbs 4:23).
- Out of your heart comes your thoughts and actions (Matthew 15:18).
- Believing rightly in your heart will make you righteous (Romans 10:9–11). In other words, place the right belief in your heart and right actions will follow.
- I have hidden your word in my heart, that I might not sin against you (Psalm 119:11).
- King David prayerfully asks the Lord to reveal anything evil in his heart (Psalm 139).

I can hardly overstate how life-changing it was to find that my beliefs, not my circumstances, determined my attitudes and actions. When I took my beliefs seriously and began to examine and change them, it did wonders for me by giving me a way to manage my emotions and form all of my actions. Look at some of the consequences of taking this belief concept into your heart and making it your own.

1. You stop complaining about everything.
2. You stop judging others.
3. You stop trying to change your mate or anyone else who bugs you, because the behavior of others doesn't control how you feel and act. This one change brings more security and safety to your mate than you can possibly imagine.

4. Instead of pointing that accusing index finger at your mate, you fold it in and point all four fingers at yourself while your thumb is pointing to God. Why? Because the only person you can change is yourself—not your mate. And changing your beliefs about what makes you happy is the beginning of life-changing wisdom.

Others determine   My beliefs determine
my happiness   my happiness

When this truth began to dawn on me, I started working only on myself and my beliefs, and my emotions and actions began to change before my eyes. No longer do I work on trying to be a better person, or changing character qualities, or putting blinders on my eyes to prevent lust. I've abandoned dependence on any outside mechanical ways of trying to change myself. I just find the beliefs that motivate my wrong actions and change them. Then it becomes a matter of watching my actions reflect my new beliefs.

The Power of Changed Beliefs

Lest you think changing your beliefs is too hard to do, let me tell you how my 10-year-old grandson, Michael, is learning this powerful truth. His mom, my daughter Kari, picked him up at school one day and asked him if he had brought all of his homework. He said he had. But after she had driven two miles, he suddenly remembered that he had left something very important in his locker.

"Mom, can you take me back?" he asked. "I left something I need for a test tomorrow, and I can't do without it."

"Michael! What is wrong with you?" Kari exploded in frustration. "Why didn't you think of this when I asked? How can you be so irresponsible? You're just like your Grandpa!" She was really at the poor kid's throat, and she kept up the verbal barrage all the way back to the school.

Little Michael said nothing. He told me later he just thought of two Scriptures: James 1:19, be quick to listen, slow to speak and slow to get angry; and Philippians 4:8, fix your thoughts on things that are true, honorable, and right. He explained that it was like he just got out of his body, sat in the back seat, and let his mom yell at his body up front.

Just from recalling these two verses changed how my grandson responded to his mom. Before he hid these verses in his heart, he would have defended himself when his mom scolded him, and the result would often be an all-out argument. But this time Michael kept his mouth shut and thought on the larger truth about his mom that stood behind what she was saying now. She fed him healthy meals, took him everywhere, kept his clothes clean, nursed him through sickness, and did more things for him than he could possibly count. In short, she loved him. This was his new focus, and it rooted out his need to get angry and retaliate against her tirade.

He told me that he "jumped" back into his body and interrupted her to say, "Mom, thank you for what you're saying to me right now, because it shows how much you love me and want me to become more responsible."

Kari's anger melted and tears came to her eyes. She told me that she felt like pulling over and handing Michael her purse, telling him to take it and buy whatever he wanted.

Just think how our world would improve if everyone began to change their beliefs and thinking in this way. No more complaining, griping, blaming each other, or escalated arguments. If a ten-year-old boy can make this principle work, so can you. Your emotional well-being should never depend on another person meeting your expectations. You can assume personal responsibility for your own moods, emotions, words, and actions simply by changing your beliefs. When this truth sinks in, you will be able to manage your feelings instead of being a victim of them. I hinted at this in chapter 3, where I discussed the futility of trying to change your mate and affirmed that the way to happiness is to change yourself. But you may have been skeptical. I understand. At first the idea does seem counterintuitive. That's why I've devoted a whole chapter to changing your beliefs. I want to convince you that promising your mate that you will change your beliefs is an extremely important step to marital security and happiness. So read on.

Most of us have little idea how much the way we are and the way we think is molded by deep-seated, erroneous *beliefs* buried deep in our heart. For example, if you believe that life should be filled with pleasures galore, you'll be unhappy anytime pleasure is denied. If you believe that trials are to be avoided at all costs, then when a big one hits you, the pain of it will be devastating and you will not be able to thank God for it and use it to grow into His likeness. What you believe impacts every area of your life, including your work performance, your attitudes about money, your emotions, your faith, and how you conduct all your relationships. Yet most of us are unaware of these hidden beliefs that guide us. The main reason we have trouble solving problems in these areas is that we address the surface emotion and the external circumstance that triggered it instead of going deeper to the belief that motivates it. The truth is that external factors don't make us happy or sad. It's what we believe about our circumstances that determine our emotions. Renowned biologist, Dr. Bruce Lipton, tells us that "beliefs are ten million times stronger in determining who we are than our thoughts." If we want to change our marriages and become happier, we must dig deep and change our belief system.

The good news is that you have the ability to change any thought or point of view you choose. When you learn to exercise that power, you can defeat false beliefs about yourself, your mate, and the world around you that keep your marriage from the happiness you desire. Harness the power of belief and you'll break through the limiting boundaries you have imposed on yourself and your partner.

For example, most men don't think they can control their lustful thoughts or avoid sexual temptations that come their way. But by changing your beliefs, you *can* control them. In a later chapter I'll tell you how I became free of lustful thoughts—a problem that plagued me all my life.

In my work as a marriage researcher, I assist couples in changing whatever holds them back from realizing God's best for their relationship. Usually they know what they want but don't know how to get there. Traditional counseling focuses on what is true now in the present moment—what skills need to be learned, and what actions need to be taken to solve a particular problem. As I've said earlier, however, learning skills and taking action are only tiny pieces of the puzzle. I have found that focusing on what people believe is vastly more effective than dissecting the stories they tell me for specific problems that need solving. Many times working on specific problems creates managed solutions without resolving the deeper problem of emotional intimacy and safety.

I began to understand the power of belief several years ago while counseling a couple whose problem was that the wife had virtually no respect for her husband. She belittled and criticized him relentlessly. She didn't feel love from him and used that to justify her nagging. I had given them new loving behaviors to practice, but nothing worked. I was at my wit's end.

Then it occurred to me that this woman really didn't care whether the marriage survived. During a session without her husband present, I confronted her, and she dismissed the idea as preposterous. "Of course I care. I want the marriage to last. Why else would I be doing all this work?"

But my words haunted her. In the next session she admitted that when she stopped denying that she didn't care about the marriage, a new insight emerged from deep inside her. Her husband had several of the same traits as her father, who was physically and emotionally abusive. And unconsciously that similarity was causing her to sabotage the marriage. Once she understood that her treatment of her husband sprang from a deep-seated belief that his similarities to her father must mean he was abusive like him, she changed the belief. She knew it was wrong and unfair. Her husband would never be abusive like her father. Within a month she stopped criticizing him and started showing unconditional respect. And the results were remarkably positive. It was all about what she had believed.

What Belief Is

Your beliefs create your view of reality. If you truly believe that your mate is trying to bankrupt you, you will tend to see and hear evidence to support your belief. If your beliefs are irrational, your view of reality will be distorted. The "reality" you see will not be the true reality, but rather a unique view of the world which seems real only for you. It makes sense why Solomon said that above everything else you ever do, guard your heart.

Your beliefs will affect your basic assumptions about who you are and what the world is like. Your beliefs will cause you to think of yourself as beautiful or ugly, worthy or unworthy, lovable or unlovable. They will cause you to see the world as either a safe or unsafe place.

You form your beliefs largely during your childhood. From the time you were born, the adults in your life passed on to you their personal view of the world and of you. What they shared, however, was really their own perception of the world seen through their own unique filter of belief. Over time and through repetition these impressions became real in your mind.

For little children, acceptance of these impressions is not by choice; it is a requirement for survival. They must have a matrix of beliefs for coping with their experiences. As the years pass, these beliefs grow stronger through reinforcement and repetition. Everything you have experienced, everything your parents, teachers, and friends have ever said to you, all the books you have ever read, and all the TV and movies you have ever watched form a lens through which you view the world— a filter of belief through which you interpret everything. According to psychologists Matthew McKay and Martha Davis, "You are constantly describing the world to yourself, giving each event or experience some label. You automatically make interpretations of everything you see, hear, touch, and feel. You judge events as good or bad, pleasurable or painful, safe or dangerous. This process colors all of your experiences, labeling them with private meanings, which become your belief system."[1]

This interpretation of life through your own unique belief system affects what you perceive to be true. Imagine that you and I are walking down the street and encounter a large German shepherd dog running loose. I love dogs. I've had several in my life, including large ones, so I believe dogs are to be enjoyed as man's best friend. You, on the other hand, were once painfully bitten by a large dog. So you believe all dogs are vicious creatures to be avoided. I whistle at the dog and call, "Come here, boy," while you look for a tree to climb. Both our reactions are based on what we believe about dogs.

Beliefs are not always products of our conscious thinking; often they lie hidden in the subconscious and affect our thinking in ways beyond our awareness. But they are always at work, always the product of all we have experienced, and always the basis for our emotions and reactions.

How Beliefs Affect Your Actions

Beliefs are so powerful that they not only change your perception of life but also how you act in response to everything that happens to you. Using your beliefs as a basis, you create rules to regulate your behavior. If your beliefs are positive, the rules telling you how to live will be realistic and flexible. On the other hand, negative beliefs about yourself and the world will produce negative rules that are irrational and fear-driven.

For example, Mary was physically and emotionally abused as a child. As a result, she formed the negative belief, *I am unattractive, unlovable, and unworthy*, which in turn produced these negative rules that govern her behavior:

1. I don't respond sexually to my husband. Who would want me anyway?
2. I don't take care of my body. Nothing I do can make me attractive.
3. I don't love unconditionally. I'll just get hurt in the end.
4. I don't express an opinion. People will find out how stupid I am.

These rules control Mary's actions and decisions in every area of her life. Her belief about herself is not true at all. She is quite attractive and intelligent. But her experiences have embedded into her mind that she is an undesirable nobody, and that belief forms her view of who she is. Have you ever known someone who glances downward or seems shy and uncomfortable in your presence? In getting to know a few shy people, I have discovered that many of them believe they are stupid, unattractive, and unworthy of being anyone's friend.

How do these deep-seated beliefs affect a marriage? Day by day, each partner filters the other's behavior through what he or she believes. Suppose you believe that your mate is responsible for meeting all your needs. What happens when your partner doesn't do this? You will react in response to what you believe should be happening. To you the situation will not seem complex or filtered or skewed in any way. Your reaction will usually be automatic and accompanied by emotion, and you will experience it simply as a spontaneous thought. But if you analyze it and trace its origin you will find that it is really an expression of what you believe.

Cognitive theorist, Aaron Beck, calls these reactions *automatic thoughts* because the term accurately describes the way we experience thoughts. As he explains, "The person perceives these thoughts as though they are by reflex—without any prior reflection or reasoning; and they impress him as plausible and valid."[2] In other words, they seem *believable*. And the reason for this is quite simple: these thoughts are based on what you *believe*. Indeed, they are expressions of your deepest beliefs. These thoughts proclaim to you how reality is put together. They describe what you know, and tell you what is real and true. In short, they describe what you *believe* about what you see and experience.

Not only do your beliefs generate your thoughts, but your thoughts reinforce your beliefs. A thought that's repeated many times can strengthen a belief to the point that it's virtually unshakable. So thoughts and beliefs form a sort of self-generating, self-reinforcing circular pattern that is often hard to break.

Changing Your Beliefs

All beliefs are based either on external, objective truth or our own natural thinking. I decided long ago to build my beliefs on God's Word, because the Bible warns us against relying on our own thinking: "There is a path before each person that seems right, but it ends in death" (Proverbs 14:12). But as God told Isaiah, "For just as the heavens are higher than the earth, so are my ways higher than your ways and my thoughts higher than your thoughts" (Isaiah 55:9). I'm sure you want to base your beliefs on God's ways and thoughts, but we often deceive ourselves and substitute our own beliefs rejecting His truth. How can you know whether your beliefs are really valid?

You must constantly examine your beliefs. You do this by working backward from your emotions, words, actions, and thoughts. Observe and listen to yourself. Step back and view your emotions as a key to understanding your deep-seated beliefs. No doubt you've often hated your emotions. "I wish I were not so discouraged," or "I hate being angry like this," or "I wish I didn't feel down so much." But remember, these emotions are not the culprit. They are neither good nor bad; they are neutral and simply reflect your deeper beliefs, which is where the real problem lies. So instead of looking at unpleasant emotions as enemies, use them in a positive way: see them as raw data telling you what distorted beliefs may exist in your heart to cause them. Trace the emotions backward to uncover beliefs that need to be changed.

Consider the case of Mitch and Susie. Mitch was two

hours late getting home. Susie greeted him with fire in her eyes, pointing her finger and yelling, "Don't think I don't know where you've been. You were with that other woman again. I just know it!" Mitch had an affair over a year ago. Even though he repented and confessed, and they were rebuilding their relationship, Susie still felt insecure. Any deviation from his routine aroused suspicions and set her off.

As Susie attacked, Mitch felt an immediate surge of anger pushing him to respond with blistering self-defense. He wanted to say, *Why do you keep ragging on me like this? That affair is in the past. How will we ever get this marriage back together if you keep hanging it on my neck all the time? You call that forgiveness?*

But instead, as she continued her tirade he did four things he had learned to do in order to change his beliefs and thoughts.

First, he paused. He remained quiet, not responding, not defending, which gave his mind time to settle. He determined not to react until he was sure that his beliefs conformed to the true reality of the situation. He focused on James 1:19: "Be quick to listen, slow to speak, and slow to get angry."

Second, he listened. He really *listened*, not just to what his wife was saying, but he listened to her heart, trying to hear what she really meant. He wanted to grasp the reality beneath her words. He wanted to understand the truth of the situation before he responded.

Third, he perceived the deeper truth he was looking for and processed it into his beliefs. *OK, what does her anger mean? She's been through a lot with me. She's endured the trauma of my affair and worked through the agonizing process of forgiving me. She wouldn't have done all this if she didn't love me. And she's proven that she does love me. She has stayed with me. She has even taken me back into her bed—she's pregnant again, about to give me another child. I have breached the security of her marriage, and she has gone through a lot of pain to repair it. Of course she gets angry when she doesn't understand where I am. She's ranting and raving because she doesn't want to go through all that again. And I don't blame her.*

Mitch's fourth and final step was to respond in a way that reflected his revamped thoughts. "Susie, I understand what you are saying. You've been through a lot with what I've done, and I can see how you would be worried when I don't show up and don't call. There was a bad wreck on the freeway, and traffic was tied up for an hour and a half. I had no way off, and my cell phone battery was dead. I'm sorry I couldn't let you know. It hurts me that you had to worry. I can see that your anger is really your love speaking. You have done so much already—taking me back into your life—and I can't thank you enough. It means more to me than I can say. You are really a wonderful woman." Then he took her in his arms and she just melted right to the floor.

This four-step process allowed Mitch to trace his emotions through his thoughts to his beliefs and adjust them right on the spot. When he did this, his new thoughts dictated new emotions. Instead of anger he felt empathy, gratitude, admiration, and love, and these emotions dictated his action. His spontaneous anger rose from his belief that Susie should not yell at him but act according to her promise to forgive. At first Mitch wanted to blame her for his negative emotions. But instead he stopped and took responsibility for his own thoughts and beliefs, making the necessary changes to produce better emotions.

When one stifles his own natural reaction to lash back, as Mitch did, he gives God's Holy Spirit a foothold in his life. Instead of letting the selfish, defensive self take charge, he allowed the Holy Spirit to take control and empower him to see his wife's heart and respond in a godlike, loving way that moved her toward security.

Most people in our world don't go through the rational process that Mitch did. And that is why their marriages, their lives, and our culture in general are in deep water. People tend to give vent to their negative emotions, which serves only to reinforce their negative thoughts. These thoughts come from beliefs that are distorted at the core. By default people believe what their fallen, natural tendencies lead them to believe. And our fallen, natural tendencies lead us to focus entirely on the self. Today's culture shows this in every way. The common focus of most people is on gathering to themselves as many things as possible to stimulate pleasure and entertainment. The common credo might go something like this: "I have a right to have *my* needs met, because my core belief is that the purpose of living is to experience pleasure. Therefore my thoughts will tend toward selfishness and immorality. Food is here for my pleasure, so I'll indulge in the tastiest fried foods, pastas, and desserts without concern for my long-term health.

Sex is here for my pleasure, so my husband, or any member of the opposite sex—or even the same sex if I prefer—is here for my use."

You can see that if everyone changed their core beliefs, our entire society would undergo radical reform. You can't change the entire nation, of course, but you can change yourself. And that alone will make a huge difference in the quality of your life. You can decide today what beliefs you will allow to remain within your heart. You can ask God to show you what your heart looks like so that you can make your beliefs consistent with His Word.

I'm sure you know people who have been knocked around by circumstance or even experienced devastating tragedies. Yet after emerging from the ordeal they retained their love for God and maintained a positive, joyful approach to life. How do they do it? They rely on their belief system, which is built on the ultimate truth that God loves them and is their ultimate source of joy and security.

Five Core Beliefs that Have Changed My Life

I have developed such a belief system for myself. It consists of five major beliefs that I store in my heart. As these beliefs become more and more fixed in my heart, I can see my actions, words, thoughts, and feelings changing me into a willing follower of what Christ called the greatest commandment: Love and serve God with your whole heart and love and serve others like you would want them to serve you. I mentally recite these beliefs day and night. The first thing I say in the morning is "Good morning, Boss (Lord)." And then I go through these beliefs and the verses connected to them. I continually add to the list of verses I'm memorizing.

1. I believe that God exists, and that He rewards me because I diligently seek after Him. I want to serve Him with my whole heart, soul, mind, and strength (Hebrews 11:6; Matthew 22:37–40).

2. I believe that God sent His Son to die for my sinful tendency to say, "I'll go my way and God can go His way." I believe that the risen Christ is now my Boss. He saved me, and now I belong to Him (Romans 10:9–10). I no longer believe that my major purpose in life is to satisfy sensual passions in pleasure. Instead, I believe I was created to be a loving servant to others (Galatians 5:13).

3. I believe that when Christ returned to the Father, God didn't leave me alone, but returned in the form of His Spirit. And He now fills me with power, love, life, and fulfillment beyond my wildest imagination (Ephesians 3:16–20).

4. I believe there is great value in all my trials, and therefore I embrace difficulties, irritations, and pain because these experiences turbocharge me into being transformed into God's image and character (2 Corinthians 12:9–10; Romans 5:3–5). Therefore,

like Paul, regardless of the circumstances, I give thanks to God in the midst of my pain. (1 Thessalonians 5:16).

5. I believe that because God loves me, saved me through Christ's death and resurrection, empowered me by His spirit, and transforms me into His image through my trials and irritations, I now have the strength and the concern to serve others in love, thus fulfilling the greatest commandment (Matthew 22:37–40).

Holding to positive core beliefs like these can change your thinking, your emotions, your responses, your marriage, and your life. They can become the basis for positive thoughts about your place and purpose in life. They can give you a higher vision of why you were created and a new way of finding joy. You will become what you believe and think in your heart (Proverbs 23:7), and you will be happier.

How Beliefs Reach Our Heart

I have read Deuteronomy 6 over and over, where Moses tells his people how to get beliefs from their mind to their heart. He says to talk about God's Word when you are at home or on a journey. Tie it to your hands and your forehead; nail it to your doorpost and your gate. The idea is to memorize verses important to you and keep them on your mind everywhere you go. I have found that I can hide God's Word in my heart by repeating verses quietly as I wake up, before eating a meal,

while driving, walking, resting, and especially just before falling asleep. I do this day and night until I see changes in my
life, then I add new verses to my list. Sometimes it may take
me an hour to go through these verses before I get out of bed
in the morning or fall asleep at night.

I love living like this because it changes my thinking and
my life. I can't remember the last time I complained about
anything. I don't gripe, judge others, and try to change people,
or retain any of the negative attitudes that used to bug me. My
love for others keeps growing, reminding me of what Jesus said:
"Your love for one another will prove to the world that you
are my disciples" (John 13:35). I diligently seek the Lord, my
Boss, and He has rewarded me with peace, low blood pressure,
low cholesterol, and many other health and spiritual benefits.

Why This Concept Is Hard to Swallow

I have found in my seminars that what I'm telling you in this
chapter is very hard for some people to grasp. They cannot
believe that happiness and contentment depend entirely on
their beliefs, regardless of what others do to them. It's much
easier to blame others for your feelings than to take personal
responsibility for them. I remember the night one man chal-
lenged me outright:

"I can't buy this at all," he said. "There's no way I'm
responsible for how miserable I am in my marriage. My wife's
nagging would make a saint miserable. If she would just stop

this one thing, I would be happy."

"No you wouldn't," I responded. "Let me explain why. Assume you are driving properly and another car bumps your car enough to cause significant damage. The other driver was negligent. He was on his cell phone with one eye on the road and the other on the open briefcase beside him. You might react in anger, chasing after the other car, cursing like a sailor, giving the driver a hand sign, and calling the police to report him. Now you'll have hassles with the insurance company, lose time at work getting estimates, have to pay the deductible, and your insurance rate will go up. You think you have a right to be angry. The whole thing is a really bad experience.

"But wait a minute. Suppose you remember your belief in God's promise that 'all things work together for the good of those who love the Lord.' You remember being taught that trials always bring blessings. Adopt this core belief in your heart and you might have an altogether different thought: 'Hey, this little auto incident will bring good things to my life in the form of godly character. It will allow me to exercise patience and kindness, thus strengthening me with more of God's power. This is all very valuable to me.'"

I know that way of thinking is totally counterintuitive. People who don't understand will think it's stupid. That doesn't matter. You are not responsible to them. You want your beliefs to align with God. His thoughts are higher than ours, and when we adopt His way of thinking, we'll find joy regardless of what goes on around us.

One of the most astounding examples of this principle at work is that of Victor Frankel. A Jewish psychiatrist in Hitler's Germany, Frankel was arrested and tortured in a concentration camp. After his death, many of Dr. Frankel's guards reported that they had never seen anyone so happy. In his own book we learn the reason: "The guards could control how much pain I was in, they could torture me, deny me food, but *they could never control my thoughts.*" He alone controlled what he believed about his destiny and what he thought of his tormentors. There is great power in controlling your thoughts. As Epictetus said, "Men are disturbed, not by things, but by the view they take of them."

If you persist in thinking the actions of others cause your unhappiness, you're doomed to remain a perpetual victim. Victims blame others or circumstances for their moods and remain unaware that they themselves have chosen to think in a manner that allows others or circumstances to control their emotions. As Victor Frankel's life demonstrates, it doesn't matter how horrible the circumstances or how terribly others treat us. We alone determine who we are by our thoughts and beliefs.

Picture Jenny and Andy. Their small group is studying a curriculum designed to improve marriages. Jenny is frustrated with Andy. She wants to work with him through the workbook exercises in the evenings. But he is dragging his feet. She practically has to force him to sit down, and when she starts reading out the questions, his responses are minimal and superficial. It's obvious he's not really into it. Finally she says,

"Can't you even spare me thirty lousy minutes to do our small group homework?"

"Honey," he replies, "I am so busy right now. You know all the stuff that's due tomorrow on that big project at work. Besides, you're turning this small group thing into a job. I've got enough jobs. We can just do this at the group meeting; they're not asking us to do homework."

"Oh, I can't believe you!" says Jenny, throwing up her arms. "What kind of idiot would be in a small group and not do the homework? We're supposed to have this stuff ready for the next meeting! She slams down the *Change Yourself, Change Your Marriage* book, scattering notes everywhere, and huffs out of the room.

"Oh, geez," mutters Andy. "Here we go again."

Okay, let's look at Andy's options. Sure, Jenny's expectations were wrong. She expected Andy to make her happy by sharing her enthusiasm. But what Jenny does is not the point. How Andy responds is what determines his happiness.

Let's assume that Andy knows the four steps we outlined in Mitch's story above. First he pauses. Instead of giving into his natural tendency to bite back, he looks at his own emotions for what they show about his beliefs. Second, he listens. He replays what Jenny said and tries to see what that reveals about her heart. Third, he tries to perceive the real truth about the situation.

Now, Mitch in the previous story was able to see the wonderful good that existed beneath his wife's anger. Andy tries the same thing. He sets aside his reactive emotion and searches for all the good he can find in his wife. Is she positive? Is she tender and loving? Is she a great mother? Is she a great cook? Is she a great lover? Is she his best friend? Does her interest in the study indicate a real desire to improve their marriage? Ordinarily going through such a list would produce several good traits in any woman.

But let's assume that it doesn't. Perhaps Jenny is a slob, a lousy housekeeper, doesn't cook, neglects the kids, never has a kind word, hates sex, pays no attention to her appearance, and does nothing but read romance novels all day. Her religion is a sham. She's a real Nazi wife. Andy can't think of one positive thing about her because it's just not there.

If that is truly the case, then Andy's life with Jenny is sure to be a trial. He can, if he chooses, do what most people do today when they encounter difficulty in marriage. *I don't need this. I have a right to have my needs met, and she's never going to meet them. I'm going to do what's best for myself and get out of this lousy marriage.* Yes, he can do this. He can take the selfish way of avoiding pain and seek pleasure instead. But he will be breaking his promise to love Jenny regardless of circumstance, and he will remove himself from the workshop God designed to mold him into a spiritual giant of faith.

Instead of choosing the easy, self-gratifying path, Andy can choose to rely on his belief as a Christian that trials produce godly character. In sticking by Jenny and treating her with unconditional love, he will be highly blessed, because each episode with his wife will be one more of God's hammer strokes to form in him the character of Christ. As James tells us, "Whenever trouble comes your way, let it be an opportunity for joy. For when your faith is tested, your en-durance has a chance to grow. So let it grow, for when your endurance is fully developed, you will be strong in character and ready for anything" (James 1:2–4).

Promise to Manage Your Own Beliefs

I urge you to solemnly promise your mate that you will con-tinually monitor your deepest beliefs and have the humility to change them when they do not conform to the truth. This promise will be a giant step in bringing security to your marriage. What does promising to manage your beliefs have to do with security? I'll close this chapter by mentioning four points to consider.

First, promising to manage your beliefs frees your mate from being a slave to your moods—from being responsible for your happiness. If you believe that your own beliefs produce your emotions, then your husband or wife does not bear the burden of having to tiptoe around your moods to protect your fragile feelings. Your mate is free to develop into the kind of person God intends.

Second, managing your beliefs reduces conflict. The four steps one takes in the face of conflicts—pause, listen, perceive the truth, and respond lovingly—virtually guarantee that conflicts will not escalate. It gives mates a platform on which differences can be amicably resolved.

Third, promising to manage your beliefs brings positive results from conflict. It gives you and your mate assurance that each conflict will result in a new examination of your deepest beliefs, coupled with a willingness to change any that do not conform to truth.

The fourth benefit of this promise is that it builds your own character. As you continually monitor your emotions, thoughts, actions, and words as a tool to understand your beliefs, you will constantly change your beliefs to conform to God's truth. This will move you toward the likeness of God Himself, enabling you to love your mate unselfishly and making you a much better person to live with.

So, make the promise. Tell your mate that you are committed to managing your beliefs in order to bring more unconditional love and greater security to your marriage.

Coming Up Next ...

The principle in the next chapter not only brings tremendous security to your marriage, it also takes pressure off your mate and offers a promise of fulfillment beyond your wildest dreams.

CHAPTER 5

I Promise to Be Filled by God

When Norma and I married we had stars in our eyes. We were in love. We just knew that our relationship would be magical forever. We would be that one couple in a million whose marriage remained total bliss. Not one person encouraged us to seek marriage training before we said our vows. We thought, like so many couples, our love would carry us through. We made the major mistake that half of all couples make: we turned each other into little gods. Well, the illusion didn't last long. How well I remember one of our first major blowouts.

During the early years of our marriage, I was finishing graduate school in St. Paul while working as a church youth minister. My salary was almost nothing. To make ends meet, Norma collected Green Stamps. You may not remember Green Stamps. As a sales incentive, stores would give customers a certain number of these trading stamps, as they were called, with every purchase. You would paste the stamps in a little booklet, and when you had enough, you could redeem them for merchandise. With each purchase at the grocery store we saved more and more stamps. Often we looked through the catalog to dream about what our stamps would get us. I had my eye on a color television, but Norma wanted a rocking chair.

Finally the day arrived when we had saved up enough stamps. While in line to trade them in, I thought I'd try once more to convince her that we really needed the television.

"Without the TV, what are you going to do while rocking in your chair?" I asked, thinking my logic was flawless. "You can get the rocker later, and the TV will give you something to do while rocking." Doesn't that make perfect sense to you? It didn't to Norma either.

"I don't want the rocker to watch TV," she said.

"Then why do you want it?" I should have stopped right there, or even better, stayed home. Because I'll never forget what ensued.

"I want it to rock our children," she said, her voice sounding so tender and nurturing.

"Children?" I said, as if such a possibility had never occurred to me.

"Yes, children," Norma smiled.

"Well, how many children do you want anyway?" I didn't know it at the moment, but at this point I needed one of those emergency pull cords that bails out fighter pilots. I was about to crash and burn! Would you believe that in all the time we had dated, even through the engagement and now marriage, I had never asked her this?

"Five or six would be nice," she replied.

"Five or six children?" I blurted.

"No—dogs," Norma smiled and punched me playfully. "Yes, of course children."

Although I was in a tailspin, I still had time to save myself. But, no!

"I don't want that many."

I wanted no more than two children. With my big personal goals for the future, I couldn't see how we could manage more than that. The other people in line certainly heard the explosion as I hit the ground at mach two. With each step toward the front of the line, Norma and I passionately debated the number of kids we were going to have. We argued until Norma finally shut down. I was humiliated, and I'm sure the other people in line were embarrassed for us. Well, what do you think we traded in our stamps for—the TV or the rocking chair? You guessed it—I'm not a complete doofus.

If you are like me, you probably said your wedding vows while harboring a whole host of romanticized ideas about love and marriage. You walked into your marriage with certain hopes and dreams, and you expected your mate to help you achieve them. You were thrilled that God had finally brought someone into your life who would meet all your romantic and emotional expectations and help you achieve your greatest desires. That certainly described me.

The Marriage Crisis in America

Most couples enter marriage hoping to achieve happiness. And for each of us, that vision of happiness takes a different form. Maybe you longed to be whole or completed. Or maybe you envisioned having perfect kids, and a family that everyone looks up to. Perhaps you hoped marriage would provide a way to live securely and comfortably, to have someone always there so you wouldn't feel lonely, abandoned, rejected, or sad. Your goal may have been to satisfy your sexual desires, for your mate to be the lover who would love you the way you always wanted to be loved. In other words, you expected to find your soul mate in your husband or wife

It may surprise you to hear me say that your marriage is in big trouble when you pursue these goals. If happiness or finding your soul mate is the objective, you are more than likely setting yourself up for failure and possibly facing years of hurt and frustration. When the marriage does not fulfill your expectations you'll wonder if there is something wrong with you or with your mate. Sadly, a person may often ask, "Did I marry the wrong person?"

Disappointment hits most couples shortly after the wedding because each partner begins to see faults and chinks in the armor of the other. That new husband or wife really needs some work. It appears that she is far from ready to meet all his needs and expectations. Instead of being sold out to her ideas of marriage, he came with his own goals—expecting her to be sold out to his. So your goal of finding happiness in your soul mate must be put aside until you change your spouse into the person you want him or her to be. You buy into the myth that will not die—that if your mate would change just a few key things, your marriage would be great.

And it's happening all around us. Marriages in America are in a horrendous mess. Although 93 percent of Americans rate having a happy marriage as one of their most important objectives in life, and more than 70 percent believe that marriage involves a lifelong commitment that should be ended only under extreme circumstances, couples marrying for the first time in the United States continue to face a 40 to 50 percent chance of divorcing, with approximately two-thirds of these divorces occurring within five to seven years of marriage. Equally disturbing is that many distressed couples never divorce, remaining in unsatisfying and/or conflicted relationships. At least one researcher suggests that fewer than half of the marriages that avoid divorce can be described as truly happy.[1]

Rutgers sociologists, Dr. David Popenoe and Dr. Barbara Defoe Whitehead, confirm these grim facts in their report on marriage titled, *The State of Our Unions—The Social Health of Marriage in America,* showing that key social indicators suggest a substantial weakening of the institution of marriage. Thanks to Hollywood characters like Murphy Brown, Grace (*Will and Grace*), Rachel (*Friends*), and real-life characters like Angelina Jolie, Madonna, and Rosie O'Donnell who celebrate the benefits of single parenthood, being a married parent is no longer viewed as the ideal for raising a family.

Could it be that marriage has been diminished to a relationship entered for the sole purpose of meeting the sexual and emotional needs of each partner? I believe that is at the heart of the problem. Today the goal in marriage is personal satisfaction. "Will *my* needs get met? What's in it for *me*?" And the biggest question of all: "Will it be pleasurable for me?" If the marriage no longer meets the personal needs of partners, they move on to the next relationship. So what's the solution? I'm convinced that once we understand and commit to God's purpose in marriage instead of using it for self-satisfaction, serious marriage problems will diminish greatly.

Though it seems paradoxical, this means if you want a satisfying marriage you've got to forget about happiness. I don't mean that you should want to be unhappy. In fact, I don't think that's possible. Everyone wants to be happy. And because we want so much to be happy, we naturally make happiness our goal and set out to find the things we think will make us happy. The problem is that happiness never comes when you make it the goal. It's like a desert mirage. It shimmers invitingly in the sunlight until you reach it, and then poof!—it vanishes. You can't go to happiness; happiness must come to you. And it only comes as a by-product of achieving a higher goal.

Happiness doesn't work as a goal, because meeting our terms for happiness depends on what happens around us. It requires just the right circumstances and the cooperation of other people. Unfortunately, those circumstances seldom align. That cooperation rarely happens. Furthermore, when a marriage is all about finding happiness, it creates dependency where we turn to our mate or require ideal circumstances to meet our expectations. And that dependency puts a heavy burden on the mate. It's true that we do have something inside that is seeking completeness and fulfillment. We all yearn to connect to a source that can fulfill all our needs. But the problem comes when we misdirect that search toward the wrong object. Your mate is not that source.

Connecting to the Power Source

On board my sparkling new party boat were my guests, a missionary family of seven. I had bragged to them about my new boat, how wonderful it was and what a great time we'd have on the lake. Now we were ready to cast off, loaded with a picnic lunch, fishing gear, water skis, and everything else needed for water fun.

Hamming it up, I told the young kids to give me a count-down. *Five . . . Four . . . Three . . . Two . . . One . . . Blast off!* I turned the ignition, and away from the dock we flew like a rocket ship from its launch pad. I overheard the five-year-old boy say to his father, "This is the coolest boat on the lake!" I loved it. I was in boat heaven. But then something happened. The engine stopped and we started losing speed.

"Don't worry everyone. I'll have this fixed in a second." I turned the ignition key several times and the engine roared back to life. Once again we were off. But then it happened again. The engine died. What was going on? This pattern of the engine starting and stopping went on for the next few minutes. I checked the gas level, oil, and anything else I could possibly think of to create the illusion that I knew what I was doing. But no matter what I did, shortly after I'd get the engine running, it would die.

"Why won't this boat work?" My voice boomed across the lake. I was completely frustrated and totally embarrassed. "Nothing is made with quality anymore." I wanted to sink that stupid boat right then and there, but I figured that drowning a missionary wouldn't help my reputation.

That's when Greg said, "Hey, Dad, what's this cord for? Every time I pull it, the engine stops." And then he started laughing. That cord was the emergency engine kill. I had been ready to blow up my boat, while all along it had been Greg playing a practical joke on me. At that moment I understood how it was possible for Abraham to place his son upon an altar.

For a boat, or anything electrical to function as it was designed, it needs to be connected to a power source. If human relationships are to function as they were designed, they, too, need to be connected to a power source. It's as if you have a built-in battery that needs daily charges to keep you feeling complete and satisfied. For a long time I believed that I could keep that battery charged, if I just plugged a 110-volt electrical cord into other people or my wife. Many of us enter marriage looking to our mate as the source of that power charge. We think, "Now that I have this person in my life, I am really going to have my needs met and be happy." We ultimately find, however, that our mates cannot recharge our battery.

Indeed, husbands and wives can be frustrating and irritating and drain away more emotional energy than they give. Our mates can be tremendous sources of help and encouragement, but if we expect them to be the source of our happiness, they are sure to disappoint us in the long run.

When coming face-to-face with this inevitable disappointment, many people assume they must have married the wrong person. Some may resort to an affair to recharge their battery. The stolen charge may light up the circuits for a moment, but after the glow fades they will feel emptier and more miserable than before. Even if they divorce and remarry the "right person," they will encounter the same frustration. The problem is not in the person they marry; it is in their expectations that that person will make them happy and keep them charged day after day. Wrong.

Sooner or later we run headlong into an inescapable fact: no person on earth is capable of giving us the fulfillment we crave. We can never plug into enough people to keep our lives filled with the happiness we want. It's no wonder so many people consider suicide as a way out. By depending on people to make us happy, we not only miss the positive emotions we crave, we also saddle ourselves with the very negative emotions we want to avoid—deep frustration, disappointment, hurt feelings, worry, anxiety, fear, unrest, uncertainty, and confusion. These emotions are the inevitable result of depending on a person, place, or thing for your fulfillment. Bottom line: We're just not wired to plug into other people as our power source.

God's Purpose for Marriage

It may surprise you to hear that God did not design marriage as a place where we can get all our needs met. In fact, nowhere in Scripture does He tell us that happiness, a soul mate, companionship, sex, or even love is the purpose of marriage. He created it with something far more wonderful in mind. God uses marriage to accomplish His primary goal for all Christians—to be conformed into His likeness. Have you ever considered your marriage to be a safe place where God can conform you to better reflect His Son? The apostle Paul explained that we are to be conformed to the likeness of His Son (Romans 8:29 NIV). This verse is not referring just to married couples, but should be the call of every believer, single, married, divorced, or widowed. But if we realize that God can use our marriage to draw us more into His likeness, the blessings will be astounding. Of course, you and I were originally created in God's image, but Adam and Eve messed that up for us. Now we get to spend the rest of our lives being transformed to better reflect His image. Marriage is one of the best tools that He uses to accomplish that.

Therefore, as we evaluate our success in a marriage our focus should not be on whether our needs are being met. Instead, we must ask, "Am I demonstrating the image and character of Jesus Christ?" We determine our success by how much we are becoming like Christ—loving and honoring our mate according to the specific roles God has laid out for us in the Scriptures. He uses the challenges of marriage to help shape and mold us into the image of Jesus. God knows that as we grow into the *image of Jesus* our deepest needs will be met, and happiness simply happens.

God doesn't want us miserable; He wants us to have life in all its fullness. As He told us, "I have come that they may have life, and have it to the full" (John 10:10 NIV). Because we have God's Spirit living within us, we are promised unlimited life, love, power, and fulfillment in Him. Who would need anything else? But we must learn that we can't have that fullness on our own terms. We were built to find our completeness only in Him. Everything starts with God. He designed us to depend completely upon Him—heart, soul, mind, and strength. He created us; He redeems us; He will glorify us. He fills us up in ways that nothing else can. We will never find ultimate satisfaction except in a vital and dynamic relationship with Him.

And how did God design us to relate to Him? In the Creation story He says, "*Let us make people in our own image, to be like ourselves*" (Genesis 1:26). God gave us certain characteristics that mimic His own so that we could communicate with Him effectively and relate to Him deeply. He desired to interact with us on a warmly personal level, to build loving relationships with us. He designed us to connect to Him, to need Him to fill us and fulfill us. As a result we remain incomplete without Him. Matthew 5:48 tells us to, "Be complete as your heavenly Father is complete." This reminds us that we are designed incomplete. God didn't intend for us to function without Him. He is the completer.

He is omni-everything; we are omni-nothing. Only through a vital connection with Him can we transcend our limitations. Without God, we find ourselves relegated to a life of unnecessary frustration, emptiness, and insecurity.

Since God made you for a relationship with Himself, the best thing you can ever do for yourself—and for your marriage—is to promise your mate that you will develop your personal connection to God through a dynamic faith in Christ. Promise that you will learn to love God "with all your heart, all your soul, all your mind, and all your strength" (Mark 12:30). You promise your mate that you will look to God to fill your life and provide you with fulfillment. This promise provides the foundation for all other promises. This is the real key to a secure, safe, and intimate marriage. Just imagine how secure our marriages would feel if our mates announced that they were focusing on knowing the God of love and finding out how to become more and more like Him. Most of us would open up willingly and give our hearts to such a person.

The 220 Principle

It's a good thing those 220-volt sockets for our clothes dryers are shaped differently than the ordinary 110-volt sockets. Otherwise people like me would try to plug a clothes dryer into a 110 plug and the resulting charge would be too low to get the job done. I would always be wearing soggy clothes. Or worse, I'd plug a lamp into the dryer socket and get myself knocked across the room.

I made a big point previously about how we humans tend to plug into wrong sources for power and fulfillment. The problem is that we're wired for 220, and we try to plug into 110 sockets. In Galatians 2:20 (not 1:10!) we find the real source for lasting fulfillment: "I am crucified with Christ, nevertheless, I keep on living, but it's not really me any more, but it's Christ living in me. The life that I now live, I live by the faith in the Son of God who loved me and gave Himself for me." The "220 Principle" means allowing Christ and Christ alone to charge us because God designed our internal batteries to be wired to His 220 current, not the 110 current of other people.

When we seek God first, happiness is no longer our goal. God is. But then a strange thing happens. We read in Matthew 6:33 (NIV), "But seek first his kingdom and his righteousness, and all these things will be given to you as well." When I put God in first place, all my deepest needs will be met. Because He loves me and actually possesses the wisdom, love, peace, and joy I've always wanted, He alone can charge my battery to full. That's exactly what He promises to do for His children:

> I pray that out of his glorious riches he may strengthen you with power through His Spirit in your inner being, so that Christ may dwell in your hearts through faith. And I pray that you, being rooted and established in love, may have power, together with all the saints . . . that you may be filled to the measure of

all the fullness of God. (Ephesians 3:16–21 NIV)

Can you be any more filled than full? Absolutely not. When I start to feel worry, fear, hurt, or any other negative emotion, I ask forgiveness for trying to plug my 220 connector into a 110 outlet—for seeking something less than God Himself. It never fails: if I expect something other than God to fill me, I feel frustration, worry, and other negative emotions. But as soon as I redirect my affections toward God, He begins filling me with the gifts that come from His Spirit. I still hold onto many expectations, but I place them all at the feet of Christ and wait for Him alone to meet them (Colossians 3:1–17). God placed deep within you an affinity for a connectedness with Him because "*he is a God who is passionate about his relationship with you*" (Exodus 34:14). It is in relationship with God that you and I find meaning, purpose, significance, completeness, inner power, peace, joy, and a relational sense of belonging. In short, there is no dream, need, aspiration, or anything else that you will ever desire that He can't meet. Period. Why? Because the almighty God of the universe created us in His likeness with the express purpose of having us know and connect to Him so intimately that we become more and more like Him. Notice the following verses:

And we, who with unveiled faces all reflect the Lord's glory, are being transformed into his likeness with ever-increasing glory, which comes from the Lord, who is the Spirit. (2 Corinthians 3:18 NIV)

His divine power has given us everything we need for life and godliness through our knowledge of him who called us by his own glory and goodness. (2 Peter 1:3 NIV)

It Is Not Good for Man to Be Alone

While it's true in the rock-bottom sense that God is all we need, He created us to relate to others as well, adding another dimension to our journey with Him. In Genesis we read that after each day of Creation God pronounced His work good. But after creating Adam on the sixth day, He found one thing that was not good: "It is not good for the man to be alone," He said. "I will make a helper suitable for Him" (Genesis 2:18 NIV). Adam's loneliness sprang from something deeper than the simple need to have living creatures around—after all, he had fawning animals by the gazillions. It was a result of having no one that was suitable for him. There was no one to complement him, and by that I mean everything from biological to complex psychological and spiritual complementation. He was the sole piece of a puzzle, designed to fit to another piece where none existed. So God created woman. After seeing Eve, the female, Adam understood this profound truth. He realized that God made male and female to fit together when He said, "together she and I are one bone, one flesh,"—in essence, one being.

However, Eve was not given to Adam as a substitute for God. He designed us to be in love with Him first, to obey His will, which was designed to lead us to life, and then to love others. Christ Himself said that the commandment above all commandments, the commandment that summarizes obedience to all of the laws of Scripture is to love God with your whole heart, soul, mind, and strength; and secondly, love others in the same way that you would like to be loved. So when we take a mate we simply extend our love for God to one other person in our life. When you promise your mate that you will open yourself to be filled by God, you are promising that he or she will be drawn into and enfolded within your love for God.

At first blush, all this may not sound altogether pleasing to you. The idea of your mate promising to look to God for fulfillment may seem to you like something of a personal rejection. If your partner's first relationship is with someone other than yourself, you may feel shut out knowing that someone other than you is first and foremost in his life. You may wonder how close and secure the two of you can really be when your first love is someone else, even if that someone is the God of the universe. After all, love triangles are deadly to marriages, aren't they?

When God is the third party in the triangle, it is anything but deadly; it is absolutely vital. Think of it in this way: Picture a triangle with God at the apex and the husband and wife at the two lower corners. If the husband and wife remain at their corners, they are at a maximum distance from God and also from each other. If the husband moves laterally along the base of the triangle toward the wife, or the wife toward the husband, they get closer to each other but not closer to God. And I've already shown how moving toward your mate, instead of God, is plugging into the wrong source of power. On the other hand, if both the husband and wife move upward along the sides of the triangle toward God, the movement automatically brings them closer to each other. The distance between them closes as they move up the triangle. Their increasing closeness with God increases their fulfillment, and their increasing closeness with each other increases their satisfaction with each other. We can see that God in the relationship is not an intrusion between the husband and wife, but rather His Spirit enables them to love each other and becomes a catalyst for drawing them together in the closest possible bond.

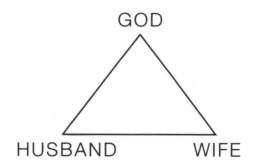

Notice that in the triangle illustration, both the man and the woman journey toward God on separate paths. The fact that in marriage a male and female become one flesh does not make them responsible for each other's journey toward Christ. Each of us is on an individual journey to become the fullest expression of who God created us to be. Each journey is unique, and each individual has different needs, desires, challenges, and obstacles to address along the way. Therefore the husband must be 100 percent responsible for his journey, and his wife 100 percent responsible for hers. Each is zero percent responsible for the journey of the other. When I stand before the Lord to give an account of my journey toward Christlikeness, I can't point to my wife and blame her for my failures. Adam already tried that, and it didn't work. "The woman you put here with me—she gave me some fruit from the tree, and I ate it" (Genesis 3:12 NIV). Neither will it work for my wife to blame Satan for her shortcomings any more than that excuse worked for Eve. Each of us is individually responsible for becoming conformed to Christ.

Yet there's another side to that coin. While marriages involve two people, each committed to their own personal journey, great marriages involve helping each other along the way. Though I am completely responsible for my own conformation into the image of Christ, God has given me this loving companion to help me get there. And I am to help her to get there. God intends for the male/female companionship of marriage to assist mates on their journey to be like Christ.

Now, here's the kicker: God built this mutual assistance of mates into the very fabric of marriage. Simply by living in a relationship, you and your mate will inevitably give each other opportunities to become more like Christ, whether or not you intend it. In fact, when one partner is committed to becoming like Christ and the other is not, each still prods the other toward Christlikeness. Here's how that works. The uncommitted mate unwittingly helps the other even through the difficult, thoughtless, hurtful, or irritating things she does, even though such actions seem the very opposite of helpful. On the other hand, the committed mate, by learning to respond to those hurtful words and actions with love and care, grows in spiritual strength, acquiring the attributes of patience, understanding, and greater wisdom. And by lovingly responding to the offending mate, the committed mate helps the other by demonstrating the loving nature of Christ, even when the partner obviously does not deserve such treatment. In fact, one of the most effective ways to show the nature of Christ is in self-sacrifice when the other person does not deserve it. That's what Christ did, and Paul tells husbands to do likewise: "love your wives just as Christ loved the church, and gave himself for her" (Ephesians 5:25 NIV). That is sacrificial love. There's nothing greater or more Christlike than that example. And when a mate is called on to demonstrate this kind of love in a marriage, the image of Christ in her takes a giant leap forward. In fact, as 1 Peter 3:1 tells us, a believing wife's honor to an unbelieving husband can be the very thing that drives him into the arms of God.

Of course, most marriages do not suffer from this kind of extreme imbalance. Yet every marriage has some imbalance, some difference between the two that causes disharmony and disruption of oneness and intimacy. Even in the best of marriages, mates do not become clones of each other; they remain unique individuals with unique perspectives. In fact, God's design for marriage assures mates of inevitable differences. The very fact that we are male and female puts two kinds of people together whose built-in orientation to life is completely different. It doesn't take long for marriage partners to realize that the masculine and feminine approaches to almost everything differ as much as the color blue differs from C sharp major. These natural differences alone produce confusion and misunderstandings that require and foster the Christlike attributes of selfless love, patience, understanding, and generosity.

In all marriages partners possess a mix of both good and not-so-good attributes, attitudes, patterns, and behaviors. Simply by dealing with them, day in and day out, each partner helps the other to grow through an exchange of both difficult irritations and loving understanding. Thus marriage becomes a workshop in which each partner is both the craftsman and the artifact. Each is the hammer and each is the anvil upon which God forges His image in the other.

Now, don't get me wrong. I don't mean to suggest that the only way marriage forges us into the image of Christ is through conflict and difficulty. Not at all. In fact, perhaps the best way in which mates can approach the nature of Christ is through simple service to each other generated solely by love. Christ demonstrated love for His disciples by serving them willingly. He didn't have to pick up that towel, fill that basin with water and wash those twenty-four grimy feet. But Jesus did it gladly, because He loved those twelve companions who had followed Him so faithfully and he wanted only the best for them. He wanted them clean. When husbands and wives stay on the lookout for opportunities to serve their mates, they find that real joy comes from bestowing this kind of honor on the one they love so dearly.

Does this mean you are to be always on the giving end and never the receiving? How can that cause you to be filled? On the contrary, it seems that it should leave you drained and empty. But that is not the case. When you recharge your batteries by plugging into Christ, He will give you more charge than you can hold. You will not only be full, you will overflow from His incessant giving. What do you do with this overflow? You pass it on to your mate. As Jesus said, "If you give, you will receive. Your gift will return to you in full measure, pressed down, shaken together to make room for more, and running over. Whatever measure you use in giving—large or small—it will be used to measure what is given back to you" (Luke 6:38). Wow! You can't outgive God. No matter how much of His love and blessing you give away, He will outdo you, refilling you so lavishly that you can't hold it all. When you become a channel for God's blessings, that enables Him to keep on giving, which in turn allows you to give back to your spouse. You keep creating capacity by passing on what you receive. Marriage partners who promise to live by this principle can lavish love on each other and yet never be empty.

Recently Dr. Bob Paul told me that there are thousands of things, people, activities, or pleasures out there just waiting to attract a person who is unfulfilled. Therefore, a marriage between unfulfilled people is highly vulnerable and anything but secure. Being filled with Christ, however, overcomes the temptation of mates to turn to these outside things to meet their needs. When one is filled with God, lesser attractions just don't seem much of a temptation. In marriage our goal is to be filled with Him and use our overflow to serve our mate. This keeps the focus of both partners within the marriage, because their attention is wholly captivated by the three-way flow of love between each other and God.

Connection with God Takes the Pressure Off Your Mate

Here is another way that your promise to be filled with God helps your mate. It takes the pressure off of him to be the one who must meet many of your needs. The pressure of having someone depending heavily on you for something you can't ever fulfill can be devastating. Imagine that you have a rare blood type, and an epidemic suddenly creates an acute need for your kind of blood. You run down to the blood bank and give dutifully, but a few days later, even before your blood has had time to rebuild, you are called to give again. You do it because you see the need, but afterward you feel the depletion of your energy. And then two days later the blood bank calls again, desperate for more. Again you do your duty, but this time you drag yourself home utterly drained. It wouldn't take many calls of this sort to do you in. You would feel pressure to meet the need, but you would not have the capacity to keep meeting it.

That's how it is with your mate when you depend on

a human relationship to fill your deepest needs. We are not designed to meet the deepest needs of each other. To depend on others for what God only is meant to supply puts impossible pressures on a relationship. Your mate can't live up to that kind of expectation, and to continue to expect such fulfillment will only cause disappointment.

As a young husband, one of my deepest needs was sex. I can remember being so irritated with Norma for not meeting that need as often as I thought she should. Arguments flared regularly. I piously backed up my arguments with 1 Corinthians 7:3, where Paul tells mates not to deny each other their conjugal rights. But all my pleading and arguing only made the problem worse. Oh, if only I had known then what I know now! Looking back I can see that I was a hedonistic man resorting to any means to convince her to meet my "need" for pleasure. The deep belief in my heart was that I had a right to pleasure. That belief needed changing—desperately.

In time that belief did change. After examining myself and turning to God for help in changing, a new belief began to take hold in my heart—I should be a servant to others through love. I began to be more understanding of Norma. I learned that women respond not to coercion (Duh!), but to unconditional love. As I learned to focus on her needs, instead of mine, I began to share my feelings, listen to her interests, praise her for who she was. I began to show her that I accepted her for what she did, and she began to open her heart and feel safe with me. In time we both began to enjoy the fullness of sexual intimacy with each other.

The key was for me to quit trying to coerce my wife and to put myself in God's hands. I needed to see that He created me to be like Him and wanted me to be transformed continually into His image by being a servant to Norma in love.

Turning to God takes the pressure off your mate. He not only fills your deepest needs, He also provides overflow by which you can help your mate on the journey. Again, we can see how promising our mate to put God first creates security in the marriage.

Oneness with God Secures Your Mate

While marriage partners are on a separate journey, becoming more like Christ creates oneness and security between them. It reduces the separateness. To picture this, let's return to the triangle illustration. As I pointed out, when the man and woman travel from their separate corners up the sides of the triangle toward God, they become closer to each other. When they reach God at the apex, they become one with Him and also with each other.

What do I mean by oneness? Ephesians 5 says that oneness is a divine mystery, something that can't be expressed in a formula or an equation. Oneness in marriage reflects the oneness that believers experience with God. It is a relationship of holy union and intimacy, "I in you, and you in Me," as Jesus put it. It is a shared life, a one-flesh relationship in which two souls and two hearts become inextricably bound together. You possess, you are possessed; you know, and you are known. You are separate fibers woven together.

The Bible gives us the ultimate expression of oneness when it tells us that, "The man and his wife were both naked, and they felt no shame" (Genesis 2:25 NIV). This is the heart of oneness, the very core of what God wants us to experience in marriage. This state of being naked and unashamed indicates that Adam and Eve were completely exposed, vulnerable, transparent, and open with one another. They hid nothing from each other. They could see each other for who they were, with all their limitations. Yet they had no shame, no guilt, no self-awareness, no fear of being completely seen and known, no fear of being rejected. The first couple experienced complete acceptance and freedom together. In other words, they were completely secure with each other. Adam and Eve could feel secure in their relationship with each other because they were already secure in their relationship with God.

We can feel that kind of security in marriage only when we root our relationship with each other in our relationship to God. When we promise to commit to Him as our source of connection and fulfillment, we enfold our mate within our relationship to God. The foundational security of this relationship allows you to open up to your mate verbally and reveal who you really are inside. It frees one mate to say to the other, "I want you to know my soul. I want to be open to you. I want to tell you who I am emotionally, psychologically, spiritually, and mentally." Dr. Paul uses a little stuffed bear to illustrate this principle. He says that if you had the capacity to unzip yourself and found that the real self inside is this little bear, you could hold it out to your mate and say, "Here is who I am—what I want you get to know and appreciate and value." Mates who feel secure with each other will be willing to unzip themselves and trust who they really are in the hands of the other. And the kind of security that fosters such intimacy is impossible, unless it's rooted in the ultimate security of a relationship with God.

You cannot coast along and expect this kind of secure oneness to happen from romantic feelings and preconceived expectations. If you do, you will grow apart. You must consciously design your lives together to achieve oneness with Christ and each other. The world will work against you, and Satan will work against you. But the oneness you achieve with each other by growing closer to God will give you security that neither the world nor Satan can breach. Here are a few simple activities that will help couples grow toward this kind of oneness:

- Pray for each other
- Pray together
- Attend church together
- Serve in some type of church or mission service together
- Eat meals together
- Read the Bible together
- Discuss together what you are learning in your quiet time

- Memorize Scripture together
- Attend a small group with other couples designed to help you grow closer together as a couple and with God

God's Authority Secures Your Mate

Promising to commit to God provides security for your mate in yet another way. It gives your marriage a solid foundation by providing a transcendent source of authority under which both of you live. A person committed to God is sensitive to His will, His rules, His design for relationships, behavior, and ethics. Promising to submit to God's authority assures your mate that you will not be guided by your own wants and whims. It means that in your treatment of the other, you will be guided by solid, unchanging, biblical absolutes rather than your desires of the moment, or by the fluctuating standards of a relativistic society.

It might surprise you to learn that Moses and I have something in common. We both love peanut butter. Well, actually it's Charlton Heston who loves peanut butter. I read somewhere that it's his favorite snack. Whether you're parting the Red Sea or mowing the yard, there's nothing tastier for lunch than a cold glass of skimmed milk and thick, creamy peanut butter spread on crackers. One Saturday morning I checked the pantry for my peanut butter before tackling my yard work. The jar was empty, but I knew not to worry; Norma was about to do her weekly grocery shopping. "Be sure and pick up a jar of peanut butter," I told her. She promised to do it.

I finished the yard and collapsed in my leather chair to cool down. When Norma returned, I was ravenous. I jumped up and pawed through the grocery bags for my precious peanut butter. "Oh, I completely forgot all about that," Norma said. "I'm sorry, honey." What should I have felt at that moment? Disappointment? Hurt? Irritation? Even rage? More important, what should I say to my wife? Not having peanut butter is hardly a big enough crisis to destroy a marriage, yet marriages have sunk on lesser shoals. Little irritations like this pop up every day in close relationships, and how you respond even to these minor things is critical, because it reveals the depth of your commitment to follow the way of Christ. "How in the world could you forget my peanut butter? I told you just before you left to get it, and you promised. What's wrong with your brain? Can't you remember even a simple thing like that?" Such a response belies your willingness to follow Christ. And it is sure to place a barrier between you and your mate, which will grow as you continue to respond this way.

If, on the other hand, you hug her and say, "Oh, that's okay, sweetheart. Don't worry about it. We all forget things now and then. I see you bought some salami. That'll do just as well," your response reflects the nature of Christ. It demonstrates that your love for her is even stronger and above the tragedy of not having peanut butter.

Even if the two of you achieve exceptional harmony with God and determine to seek His will in everything, this does not mean that you will never disagree. But it does mean that when those disagreements occur, you are committed to seeking the truth in a loving, open, and considerate way rather than resorting to your own subjective standards. When your mate sees that you are following God's rules for love and life rather than making them up as you go, he or she will feel much more relaxed, *more secure and safe* knowing you are committed to a power higher than yourself. Promising to put God at the foundation of your marriage provides the most solid security possible.

As you can see, the benefits of promising your mate to love God first are many: It plugs you into the proper source of fulfillment; it fosters oneness; it takes the pressure off your mate to fulfill all your needs; it gives you overflow from God's blessings to pass on to your mate; it secures your mate under God's authority; and most importantly, it transforms you into the image of Christ.

As to the downside to making this promise . . . there isn't any.

Coming Up Next...

Did you know that you can keep the bad things that happen to you from being really bad? Most people don't. But it's not only possible, It's a healthy way to live. I'll show you how in the next chapter.

CHAPTER 6

I Promise to Find God's Best in Every Trial

*E*arly in our marriage my wife, Norma, had a habit that irritated me out of my gourd. She smacked her chewing gum. I couldn't stand it. It was even worse when the two of us were cloistered together in the car, especially on a long trip. We'd be driving down the freeway and she'd be engrossed in a book or watching the scenery, and her gum would be smacking, smacking, smacking. The hair on my arms stood straight up. I would endure it as long as I could, but when I could take no more I'd remind her gently that she was again doing this disgusting thing I had pointed out to her many times before:

"Honey, you're smacking your gum again."

"Well, I'll stop smacking my gum when you stop stuffing your fingers in your mouth," she retorted.

"What do you mean? I never stuff my fingers in my mouth!"

"Oh, come on," she said. "You suck on your fingers all day long."

"Maybe my mom stopped nursing me too soon," I responded.

But my humor fell on deaf ears, and that really pushed my irritation buttons. So off we went into battle. Sure, I bit my nails now and then, but what's such a big deal about that? It's not like she has to listen to it all the time.

If you can believe it, things have changed greatly between us since then. Now when she does some little something to irritate me, I can actually hold my tongue and start working on myself instead of pushing her to stop her behavior. We have both added a lot of security to our marriage by actually becoming grateful for the things that irritate us instead of trying the age-old fruitless effort of trying to change each other. In this chapter I'll show you how I made that change.

Splinters, Specks, and Logs

We humans are strange creatures. Often the very thing that irritates us in others is similar to something we do ourselves. Why are those minor faults of my wife's so obvious to me while mine are so hidden? I can see two reasons. First, it's easier to excuse myself than to excuse others. Sure, I have this annoying little habit of biting my nails, but I'm under a lot of pressure, you see, and it calms my nerves. I have a reasonable excuse for doing what I do. But there's no excuse for her smacking her gum. How does that help anything? She could easily close her mouth while she chews. The second reason I focus on her faults instead of mine is that subconsciously I know my behavior needs correcting. But I don't want to open that can of worms. When my behavior scrapes against hers and causes friction, it's a lot easier to correct her behavior than to change mine.

Sometimes the problem is even worse. We get bent out of shape over a very minor fault in our mate while harboring in our own life a major fault that we ignore. Jesus noted this tendency when He said:

> Do not judge, or you too will be judged. For in the same way you judge others, you will be judged, and with the measure you use, it will be measured to you. Why do you look at the speck of sawdust in your brother's eye and pay no attention to the plank in your own eye? How can you say to your brother, "Let me take the speck out of your eye," when all the time there is a plank in your own eye? You hypocrite, first take the plank out of your own eye, and then you will see clearly to remove the speck from your brother's eye. (Matthew 7:1–5 NIV)

Jesus knew us pretty well, didn't He? You see a little speck of sawdust (like smacking gum) in your mate's eye can bug you to no end. You make it your job to get that thing out of there. But all the while you have this big plank, or maybe even enormous logs stuck in your own eye, and you don't even notice them. Do you know what else I think Jesus was telling us? *You have enough logs in your own eye to keep both you and Me busy. Let's just work on changing you until you look more like Me. That'll take at least one lifetime.*

I have spent far too much energy trying to pick tiny bits of sawdust from my wife's eye. During the first part of our marriage, I tried to fix every little thing Norma did that irritated me. As I've said in previous chapters, changing your mate does not work, and I think I've finally learned that lesson. Today I'm no longer interested in changing Norma. Notice I'm not saying that I don't want her to change. I do want her to continue to grow in her relationship with God, with others, and with me. But I have learned that even my best efforts will not change her. People can't change people; only God can change people. Of course I can, and should, influence others by my behavior and by making changes in myself. I also have a moral responsibility to encourage others to change their behavior if I see them doing something illegal, rude, or belittling. But as a rule I never suggest that others change any aspect of their life unless I'm invited to do so. I must have permission, or my attempt to help is really an invasion of their personhood. The only person I have a right to work on is myself.

And the truth is, that self of mine needs work. Lots of it. And that persistent urge I have to fix those little irritating flaws in my wife really reveals just how selfish I am. I may try to convince myself that my motives for fixing her nagging and carping are "for her own growth and good." But the truth is, it's not really about her. It's really about my comfort and me.

I want my life to be easier and more pleasant. So instead of looking at myself and trying to determine what there is about me that might possibly cause all that nagging and carping, I take the easy, selfish road. I try to get her to change, so I won't have to go through the rigors of self-examination.

Whenever your focus is on what the other person is doing, you take away your own power. You demonstrate that you believe you can't do anything about an irritating situation yourself. It's up to the other person to do it. In focusing on the other person, you put the solution to the situation into the hands of another, thus losing control. It's an exercise in futility and ineffectiveness. If, on the other hand, you look to yourself, then you have power to find a solution. You can control yourself. Could that be why Jesus urged us to attend to the log in our own eye?

Judgment-Free Zones

Looking at the logs in your own eye before removing the speck from your mate's eye is highly critical to the well-being of your marriage. And the reason is quite simple: judgment destroys security. The mate who is always having his eyes examined for specks will have the sense of being under constant scrutiny. He will feel pressure to measure up in order to keep the love of his wife. The message is, "If you want me to continue loving you, you'd better get rid of that irritating habit." This does not express unconditional love, and it's hardly the way to create security in a marriage. Security comes from knowing your mate will love you regardless of your flaws and shortcomings. Real love is unconditional.

If love is unconditional, there's no need for judgment. That's why James challenges Christians to conduct all their relationships in judgment-free zones when he says:

> Brothers, do not slander one another. Anyone who speaks against his brother or judges him speaks against the law and judges it. When you judge the law, you are not keeping it, but sitting in judgment on it. There is only one Lawgiver and Judge, the one who is able to save and destroy. But you—who are you to judge your neighbor? (James 4:11–12 NIV)

Who is the only one with the right to judge? God. So, what are we doing when we judge? We are playing God, as if we were perfect as He is and had no logs in our eyes. Judgment is unhealthy, not only to our marriages, but also to ourselves. Psychology researchers, Childre and Martin, have reported that as soon as judgmental words come out of your mouth, deadly chemicals are released into your bloodstream. These chemicals weaken your immune system and disrupt the balance between your heart and your brain. "Negative judgments simply aren't healthy," they write. "Like other deficits, they create stress and incoherence in your biological systems. All those negative [judgmental] attitudes and feelings running through your body are toxic, and they shut off the riches of the heart. . . . *The person who judges is the one who's hurt the most"* (italics mine). [1]

Judgmentalism damages marriages because it allows a destructive force into the relationship that should be permanently locked out. We can endure criticism and judgment from the outside, but when those things come from a mate, the security of the marriage is shattered. Your home can be a haven where love and trust flourish only if you make it a judgment-free zone.

Judgment-free zones are created when you forget the sawdust speck in your mate's eye and realize the presence of the log in your own. Then go to work removing it. You will be surprised at the practical effect of doing this. Logs in one's eyes—that is, blindness to your own faults—are a core cause of conflict in marriage. If you understand and act on the log principle, it will change your life and your marriage. As I will show you in this chapter, focusing on your own logs and taking steps to remove them will give you the power to end all escalated arguments. Is that a great promise or what?

Using Irritations to Identify Logs

The things your mate does that irritate you often reveal your blind spots—the logs in your eye. Analyzing your irritations will often spotlight the things in your life that need to be changed.

Jerry is really getting put out with Sarah. In the mornings she's sulky, short-tempered, and irritable as he hurries about shaving, tying his tie, gathering his laptop and briefcase, while she plods about in her housecoat, hair rumpled, nursing their baby daughter and wiping the nose of their toddler son, who is scattering plum jelly about the kitchen from his high chair. As he leaves for work Sarah avoids the goodbye kiss and says, "You go off to work and have a great time, and I'll just stay here with the kids and go insane." Jerry says nothing, but he seethes inside at her sarcasm. *What do you expect? It's 7:30 in the morning. Normal husbands go to work.*

Then to make matters worse, every evening at about 4:00 Sarah starts calling him at the office, asking when he'll be home for dinner. *She wants me to work only twenty hours a week. And during those twenty hours she expects me to think of nothing but home.* Her snide little comments are driving him up the wall. Last week when she suggested that he was too wrapped up in his work and spent too little time with her and the kids, he exploded.

"I've got to make a living, don't I? How do you think we pay for this house, the car—and all those expensive outfits you went out and charged last week?" *Geesh! That woman wants to control me like a robot. She expects me to do whatever she wants every waking moment of the day.* If she would just do her job of taking care of the kids and let him do his, he could get on up the corporate ladder and they'd all be better off, right?

What is bugging Jerry? He wants to be the man—the hunter/provider—and he expects Sarah to be his cheerleader and bless him with a great sendoff every day, as the mighty hunter marches out in pursuit of his quarry. But she's not doing it. Furthermore, she's trying to control him with all her complaints and pouting and cutting remarks about his neglect of his family. And that irritates him to no end. He sees it as a flaw in her character—a splinter in her eye that needs to be taken care of.

Fortunately, however, Jerry is a Christian who takes God seriously and wants to draw closer to Him. So on his half hour drive to work he starts thinking. He remembers James 1:19, which says if you're quick to listen, you'll be slow to anger. And he understands that "quick to listen" doesn't mean you should get the listening over with as fast as you can. It means slow down and listen until you understand. And understanding tends to displace anger. So he decides to try to listen for what might lurk beneath Sarah's irritating behavior. What does she do that makes him think she's controlling? Well, she lays a guilt trip on him when he leaves in the morning and if he's not home by 5:30. She bugs him to be home more. When he's home she wants the family to dominate his time. Yep, Jerry determines. *No doubt about it, she's controlling.*

Then suddenly another verse comes to Jerry's mind: "When you say they are wicked and should be punished, you are condemning yourself, for you do these very same things" (Romans 2:1). *Who me? I'm not doing the same thing. I'm not controlling. I'm just trying to break free of her attempts to control me. All I want from her is a little help and encouragement as I try to make a life for us.* Then the truth hit him like a blitzing linebacker. Sarah was also trying to make a life for them—a life based not on financial security, but on family security. That's when he saw it: this huge, ugly log hanging from his eye. It had blinded him to the truth about himself. He was being self-centered. He was irritated because Sarah wanted to control him, when in reality he was the one controlling Sarah, using her as a prop for his own personal goals of advancement.

The moment Jerry got to the office he called Sarah and asked her forgiveness for not recognizing his blind spot. When Jerry took steps to remove his log, that changed not only him, but Sarah also changed. As soon as she began to feel like the top human priority in Jerry's life, she relaxed. With family security reestablished, she quit her carping. Not only that, but the implied promise of delicious morning send-off kisses made him want to get home in the evenings as fast as he could.

As Jerry's story demonstrates, that which irritates you often points to a log in your eye. A log hanging out of your eye naturally skews your perception of reality. It blocks your vision and keeps you from seeing the needs of your mate. You interpret those needs as irritations. Taking the time to probe honestly for the truth behind those irritations allows you to see that you have a blind spot—a log in your eye—a problem in your life that needs attention. Paul tells us in 1 Corinthians 7:28 that if you marry you will have problems. But we can turn those problems into good things if we use them to make us more like Him day after day. Marriage can become the "wood chipper" to get rid of those logs. One purpose of marriage between two sexes with their innately different and sometimes frustrating ways of looking at life is to make each partner more like Christ. The irritations caused by these differences act as sandpaper, smoothing out the rough edges. So thank God for the ways your mate irritates you!

Even after I learned this principle I didn't always handle it very well. Sometimes when Norma did something that irritated me, I would say, "Thank you very much for correcting my driving. I really needed that today so I could keep growing in Christ." You can imagine how that went over. I soon realized that spouting off this way was just another form of self-righteous piety. The better way was to keep my mouth shut and thank God silently.

From Selfishness to Service

Every log in your eye grows there from the seed of selfishness. We have these blind spots because we don't like self-examination. We know that once we start a process like that, there's no telling where it will end. All kinds of changes will have to be made, including dethroning our self and making Christ the Lord of our life.

Of course, we like to say that we want Christ to be the Lord (boss) of our life, but we don't like to do what is necessary to make that happen. We don't like giving up control of ourselves—or our mates. Giving up control is hard. Dethroning self and putting God first is even harder. Many say the words, but few accomplish the feat. We desperately clutch our logs because, deep down, we *want* that blind spot. We want to keep that log in place as an excuse for not seeing the truth about ourselves. It keeps us from looking at our need to make a real change.

We resist relinquishing control because we think that having to do what another wants instead of what self wants will make us unhappy. We have trouble letting Christ take the wheel, because His ideas about happiness may not mesh with our own. But if we allow Christ to have control, He promises to lead us into joy.

When I made the decision to change and began to act on it, my wife changed. As I will explain in a later chapter, the moment she felt in her spirit that she was first in my life, she began encouraging me in my ministry opportunities. When I removed the log from my eye, she took it on herself to remove the little specks from her own eye.

You see, the fact that I chose to focus on my own blind spot didn't mean that Norma had no blind spots of her own. It's seldom a matter of one partner being all right and the other being all wrong. Like any human, Norma had her faults. She was an only child, the princess of her home, doted on by her mother and father. She was the focus of attention and could do no wrong. With no brothers or sisters to disrupt her plans or sap the family budget, she had order, financial security, and regularity in her life. Therefore, when I entered the scene, my failure to place her at the center was worse for her than it might have been for a woman with a different upbringing. That, along with my chaotic schedule, robbed her of her accustomed security, and thus her reaction was extreme. That was the speck in her eye.

But the speck in your partner's eye is not your responsibility. When we hear a convicting sermon it's our tendency to elbow our mate, as if to say, "Are you listening? Did you get that?" But that's not the way to do it. The sermon is always about you, never the other person. You can change only yourself. Yet when one partner takes responsibility for his own logs, it changes both partners, and therefore it changes the marriage. When I changed, Norma took responsibility for her own blind spot and changed as well. This is the way it almost always works. I call it the Dance of the Lumberjacks—two people celebrating their oneness by working hard on their own logs.

Rooting Out Your Logs

The process of using irritations to identify and remove logs from your eye is similar to that of changing your beliefs, which I outlined in chapter 4. I'll go through the steps briefly.

First, when your mate does or says something to irritate you, pause instead of striking back. Stifle your natural impulse to complain or to remind your partner of how many times you've asked her to stop doing that. Give your mind time to settle and get calm.

Second, listen to what your mate is saying. Don't just listen to the words; listen to the heart. Are her words and behavior symptoms of a deeper problem? Try to find the reality beneath the words in order to understand why she continues to say them.

Third, look at yourself. *Does the irritation I feel because of my mate's behavior indicate a log in my eye? Do I have a blind spot? Is it possible that I am doing something to cause my mate to keep ragging on me like this?* Make an honest assessment of your own behavior. Make no assumptions that you are in the right, but to the contrary, assume for the moment that you have a problem that you don't see clearly. Be hard on yourself. Try to adopt your mate's point of view and see yourself as he or she might.

Fourth, root out the log. Change your behavior. Get rid of your selfishness and adopt a humble servant's heart. Can't do it? Don't be surprised, because you are utterly helpless to change on your own. Humble yourself before God and cry out to Him like a helpless baby bird in the nest calls out to the parent that can feed it.

"God, I'm having real trouble giving up my own wants and becoming a servant to my mate. That person you gave me is irritating me like fingernails on a blackboard, and that's sure evidence that I have a log. Grab hold of it with me. Let's rip it out of there so You can make me more like You. My purpose in life is to reflect You. Let my mate be a woodcarver, helping chip away my logs, so I can grow into Your likeness."

And the very best way to change behavior is to let God's Word, hidden in your heart, change you. Find words like Romans 5:3–5 and repeat them over and over as God told His people to do in Deuteronomy 6:7–9, until you have His counsel safely hidden in your heart.

Breaking Log Jams with Forgiveness

When you don't get rid of logs, bad things can happen. Logs can jam up and clog the flow of love in the relationship. Mere irritations can swell into major problems that inflict serious pain and anguish on marriage partners. Mates who don't work on their logs often allow these log jams to create eddies and whirlpools of bitterness, anger, or resentment. Mere irritations can rise to the level of real offenses that may be hard for the offended mate to release and forget. Unless these offenses are resolved, they can eat away at the mind and heart.

When unresolved irritations and logs cause damage to our relationships, one step is necessary before the relationship can resume, and that is forgiveness. Forgiveness is crucial to maintaining a marriage. Forgiveness opens the door for repair and reestablishes security. When mates forgive they show their commitment to remain connected. Therefore, one of the best promises you can make is that you will always be quick to seek forgiveness and quick to forgive. Without forgiveness, you're not likely to make it to your fifth wedding anniversary, much less to your fiftieth.

What makes forgiveness so important? Well, aside from the impossibility of maintaining a marriage without it, forgiveness makes us more like God. It also improves our physical and emotional health. And it keeps security alive and well. Failure to forgive bottles up the acid of bitterness, anger, resentment, and vengefulness that can grow inside of you. It's like drinking poison and hoping the offender will get sick. It's nonsensical. It does nothing to hurt the other person, but it destroys you. Sure, a person can be offended when you do not extend forgiveness, but you are the one who ultimately suffers. You may try to bury your bitterness or anger without resolving the offense. But you never bury anger dead; you always bury it alive. And it forms acid puddles deep in your heart, stagnating, festering, eating it away like an infection. Soon something like gangrene sets in. That's why the apostle Paul tells us, "Get rid of all bitterness, rage, anger, harsh words, and slander, as well as all types of malicious behavior. Instead, be kind to each other, tenderhearted, forgiving one another, just as God through Christ has forgiven you" (Ephesians 4:31–32). Forgiveness is for your own good.

The word *forgiveness* combines two ideas. One is to erase, or untie knots. The other is restoration. When you forgive you untie the knots put into the relationship by an offense. When I fail to resolve relationship issues, knots and tangles of resentment and bitterness thicken in my subconscious mind. They ensnare me and tie me up, and I'm unable to move into freedom and joy. The moment I forgive you, God unties these tangles and frees my heart. Then I am released into His grace and power, free to love Him, others, and myself.

In another metaphor, when you forgive you erase the offending incident from the relationship's story. You go to the marker board and completely wipe away all the wrongs done to you. Whatever your mate did is now nothing. The board is blank. The issue is not there any more. That's what forgiveness means. Thus the offending mate is released from carrying guilt and relieved of all the baggage of bitterness, resentment, and anger that can weigh one down in response to offenses.

The greatest benefit of forgiveness is that it makes us more like God. God is the great Forgiver. He has forgiven all of us from every sin that we ever committed—and that's a staggering load. He tells us that the forgiveness we receive should be passed on to others. In fact, He says, in effect, that we qualify for His forgiveness by passing on His forgiveness to those who need our forgiveness. The truth is, you have been forgiven of tons of sins during your lifetime. Have you ever turned around and refused forgiveness to someone who wronged you? Big mistake. Matthew 18:23–35 tells what can happen to you. In this parable Jesus tells of a king settling accounts with his servants. He forgave a man who owed him ten thousand talents, which was equivalent to millions of dollars in Jesus' day. But then that forgiven man went out and immediately demanded payment from a fellow servant who owed him a mere hundred denarii (Just a few bucks!). When the fellow servant couldn't pay, the forgiven man had him thrown into prison. But when the king got wind of what this forgiven man had done, he called him back in and turned him over to jailers to be tortured until he paid his debt in full. The man's failure to show mercy cancelled the king's mercy to him.

I am that unmerciful servant. God has forgiven me of all my sins, and that required some really heavy-duty forgiveness. It's when I forget about how I have been forgiven that I fail to forgive others. How ungrateful! Jesus actually said in this parable that our Father in heaven will not forgive us unless we forgive others. Forgiveness is the cornerstone of following Christ.

Barriers to Forgiveness

As important as forgiveness is, it is often very hard to do. If the damage to the relationship is significant, the offended mate may want to forgive, but he or she will find barriers that will hinder them from actually doing it. These barriers are sometimes quite hard to surmount, but they must be surmounted if the marriage is to survive. Let's look at some of the common barriers to forgiveness that couples are sure to encounter.

A Closed Heart. Jim and Beth had been married for seven years when Beth discovered that Jim was having an affair. She was devastated. But Jim stopped seeing the other woman and seemed truly repentant. He begged Beth to forgive him and take him back. After recovering from the initial shock, she decided she wanted to repair the marriage, partly for the sake of their two children. But it wasn't as easy as she had hoped. She came into my office greatly troubled.

"I want to forgive Jim," she said, "but I just can't seem to let it go. My feelings swing back and forth. One moment I feel hurt, rejected, worthless, and unattractive, like I'm a failure. Why else would Jim go to this other woman? Then the next moment I'm angry as a hornet, wanting to scream and tear his head off for doing this terrible thing to me."

"It sounds like you're not only hurting; you also seem to feel helpless," I said. "You want to forgive, but you can't do it because all these vulnerable and angry feelings keep getting in the way."

"Yes, that's it exactly," Beth replied. "Saying I want to forgive is easy—sort of. But when it comes to actually doing it and knowing I've done it—I just can't seem to get there."

"What holds you back?" I asked.

"Well, I keep thinking if he did it once, he could do it again."

In light of the principles we've studied so far in this book, we can understand Beth's anguish. The security of her marriage has been breached, and she no longer feels safe. She has also been dishonored. Her husband has failed to lift her up as the most precious possession in his life. And in these failures he has deprived her of two of the most crucial elements of a stable marriage—security and honor. The heart of the relationship has been ripped out, because he made a commitment and broke it. Beth feels adrift, insecure, unsafe, uncertain, dishonored. It's no wonder her emotional pendulum swings continually from anger to vulnerability. She doesn't know where to turn for security.

"Beth," I said, looking her straight in the eye. "Do you want to know why I think you're having trouble forgiving Jim?"

"Oh yes, please tell me," she said.

"It's because your heart is not open. Fear is causing your heart to close against Jim. You are afraid that because he did this thing once, he might do it again. You are letting him control your emotions instead of taking control of them yourself."

"But this is a marriage," she replied. "We're supposed to depend on each other for love, honor, and security. That's what we promised in our wedding ceremony."

"That is true," I responded. "But we humans fail each other. We are fallen, and we are weak, and we succumb to temptation and let each other down. That is the very reason that we cannot allow our happiness to depend on another person—not even a husband or wife. Not even if ironclad vows have been made and sealed with rings and kisses. You must face the fact that you are always responsible for your own feelings. The better you get at taking care of your feelings, the less you will need Jim to do that for you. If you learn to take care of your feelings and manage your pain, then even if Jim hurts you again, it will be painful, but you can still be okay. You must reach a point where your feelings, your happiness, your deepest security does not depend on him.

"Once you adopt this attitude, you can take whatever good Jim gives you as a gift and enjoy it without making it an absolute necessity to your well-being. Do this and it will free you to forgive him. It will put control of your happiness in your own hands, and this will allow forgiveness to come much easier."

"How do I get to that point?" she asked.

"You must get filled up by God," I told her. "You must find your deepest security in Him." Then I explained to her the principles I've given to you in chapter 4 of this book: how a relationship with God is our only source of real security.

Now, in telling Beth these things, I was not helping her to restore the marriage. At least, not directly. The principle of taking responsibility for one's self only lays the foundation for restoration. Restoring the marriage means taking certain steps of repair. But repair can't begin without forgiveness; forgiveness can't happen without an open heart; and hearts can't be opened until fear is removed. Beth will feel free to forgive Jim when her heart is open. Your heart opens as you realize how much *you* have been forgiven, and when you allow God to use your pain to transform you into more of His image. Resentment fades as the treasures of God's character slowly seep into your heart and reform your behavior.

Jim showed that his heart was open to repair the marriage when he took ownership of the pain he had caused and sought forgiveness. But if Beth thinks her ultimate well-being is still dependent on him doing the right thing, her heart will close and Jim's plea will fall on deaf ears and paranoid fears. As long as she depends on him for her happiness, she can never forgive because she can never be certain. Hearts open up only when they feel safe and secure. But as important as it is for husbands and wives to create security for each other, we are imperfect in our ability to provide security. We will never feel truly secure until we root our security in our relationship to God.

Every time I go through this with anyone, the response is, "Wow! You mean if I learn to take care of my own feelings and become confident in my relationship to God, I can manage my pain and get to a good place? Then even if he hurts me again, I can still maintain my equilibrium and come out okay?" Yep, that's what I'm saying. People who root their security in God find themselves free to forgive and restore their damaged relationship. My mate may fail me because she is a fallen human being, just as I am. But God will never fail me. He forgives me when I need it, so why shouldn't I forgive others?

Anger and Resentment. These ugly twins are huge barriers to forgiveness. It is impossible to have an open heart and be receptive to God's will if we are in serious conflict with others. God desires our lives to be a sincere gift to Him, not tarnished with unreconciled differences or clogged with bitterness from past hurts. Jesus was quite explicit about this: "So if you are standing before the altar in the Temple, offering a sacrifice to God, and you suddenly remember that someone has something against you, leave your sacrifice there beside the altar. Go and be reconciled to that person. Then come and offer your sacrifice to God" (Matthew 5:23–24). Our worship to God is meaningless until we make sure that people we have offended, or people we've been offended by, are freed from the bondage of anger, vengeance, or hate. When we free them, we free ourselves.

If you're on the verge of being angry all the time, and your mate or your family has to tiptoe around as if stepping through a mine field wondering which misstep will set off an explosion, you are doing them a great disservice. You may believe that what they do is the cause of your anger. But that is dead wrong. Your anger comes from inside you. Blaming your mate or your family for your anger makes them falsely responsible for it and allows you to evade responsibility that should be yours alone.

You have a log in your eye. It's your own beliefs and thoughts that provoke your anger—not the actions of people around you. You are the one who needs to beg their forgiveness. You need to sit down with your family and your mate and say, "Look, I've been really angry with all of you. I blamed you for it, and you probably accepted the blame much of the time. But I've learned it has nothing to do with you. My anger came from myself—from my own thoughts and beliefs. You were just an excuse for me to pull the trigger. I take full responsibility. I am so sorry that I've made you live in this minefield."

Now, before you get the wrong idea about anger, I want to explain that it is not always bad. "Be angry and yet do not sin" (Ephesians 4:26 NASB). Anger is so often abused that many Christians link it with sin. Anger is merely an emotion, and like all emotions, there's nothing wrong with it in and of itself. Positive anger lets us know something needs to be taken care of. It's like the red warning lights on your dashboard. When they're blinking, you'd better take notice or you'll end up on the side of the road with a steaming radiator and your thumb in the air. It's right to get angry at an injustice or when someone is trying to hurt your family. Anger motivates us to take appropriate action. Like dynamite, it has useful purposes, but it's so explosive that it needs extremely careful handling to keep it from destroying us.

If we misuse anger to defend our wrong beliefs and thoughts, or if we let it take root and hide it inside our heart where it can emit resentment or thoughts of revenge, we set ourselves up for a great deal of harm. When we hold onto anger it ferments into hate, which is a toxic waste in our soul that blocks our relationship with God and our loved ones. Pent-up anger will build pressure in your soul and explode unexpectedly to hurt the people around you.

We like to justify our anger as being "righteous indignation," but be honest. Most of your anger can make no pretense of being righteous. You get angry because you're self-centered. Your anger is a reaction to not receiving what you expected from other people or circumstances. There is nothing righteous about it; it is a blatant assertion of self. Your little ol' finite self is all hacked because you're not getting your way. You believe that life is for pleasure or excitement, and it's not happening for you. So you put your little thumb in your mouth and you're hurt, you can't find your blankie. So you kick your legs in the air and scream. And you're going to keep throwing your tantrum until you get your way. Sorry to put it so bluntly, but that's exactly what most of our anger really is. It's a 38-year-old's way of acting like a four-year-old.

Or instead of the temper tantrum, you may do the adult equivalent of pouting. You've been hurt, and you're ready to feel like a victim. The signs are depression, listlessness, isolation, or bitterness. When we experience these emotions it's only natural to want to medicate them. It's the human way to ease emotional pain. We turn to drugs, alcohol, food, or anything that makes us feel better. But these "cures" are only momentary. Only one thing can cure your bitterness and move you toward maturity and health. You must forgive or seek forgiveness. Otherwise, you will slide into the dark, acid pit of unresolved anger.

Ephesians 4:26–27 says, "Don't sin by letting anger gain control over you. Don't let the sun go down while you are still angry, for anger gives a mighty foothold to the Devil." Forgiveness is critically important as the valve that allows pent-up anger to vent into oblivion. Forgiveness says, "I know you're not perfect, but neither am I. I choose to love you anyway and to forgive you so that I am free to grow in the magnificence of God."

Forgiveness is essential, but it doesn't come naturally for us. Forgiving, and especially seeking forgiveness, hurts our pride. It means dropping our defense of self and adopting an attitude of humility. That's not easy, but you can't find peace until you do it. God gives His grace only to the humble. A humble person submits to God and strives to become like Him by following His way. God forgives—does He ever forgive! And to become like Him, we must do the same.

Make the Promise

Promise your mate that you will accept all the negative things that happen to you as opportunities for personal growth. Promise that you will use both the little irritations that are inevitable in every marriage, as well as the major traumatic hurts and suffering, to learn about yourself and discover your blind spots. Promise that once you identify these blind spots—those logs in your eye—you will call on the power of Christ to root them out.

Promise this dear person in your life that your love is stronger than his or her faults. He is a treasure you will honor and love in spite of his faults. She is more precious to you than anything in your life, even if she does have a few flaws. Therefore you will always focus on your mate's value instead of her weaknesses.

Further, admit that because of your own weaknesses, you know you are going to hurt your mate from time to time. Promise sincerely that you will always repair the breach by seeking forgiveness. Promise that you will also forgive, no matter what. Such a promise will cause a multitude of sins, hurts, anger, resentment, vengeful thoughts, and bitterness to evaporate as if they never existed.

These promises will give security to your mate in two ways: 1) You will not expect perfection from your partner, but will love him or her in spite of the flaws you find. 2) You will take responsibility for yourself and pry the logs from your own eye instead of looking for grains of sawdust in your partner's eye.

These are promises worth making . . . and keeping.

Coming Up Next...

Imagine being married to a person who says, "Honey, from now on, I want to help you win every argument we have, no matter what issue we are facing." Impossible? Not at all if you learn just the few basic principles of loving communication that produce harmony and oneness in marriage. You'll find these in the next chapter.

CHAPTER 7

I Promise to Listen and Communicate with Love

In my interviews of well over 60,000 women all over the world, I've learned that no matter what the culture, the economic level, or the geographic location, all have one thing in common: the need for conversation. I ask them all the same question: "What would improve your marriage?" I get the same answer time and time again: "If my husband would just talk to me more and share his heart, our marriage would improve."

"What do you mean by talk and share his heart?" I ask.

And the answer is always the same: "I just wish he would listen and respond and understand when I share my feelings and not try to fix me or the situation."

"You're saying that if you had better, more meaningful communication with your husband, your marriage would improve?" No matter what country I am in, the answer is always, "Yes!" All over the world women complain that men do not talk to them enough. And when men do talk, they don't hear what women are really saying.

As I continue asking this question, the new twist I keep hearing from women is this: "When my husband talks with me, I feel secure. And that rates a ten to me."

Do you find it odd that in a world with two sexes obviously designed to be together, there is a universal communication problem between them? How did such a thing come to be?

It all starts before birth when our brains are being formed in the womb. Both male and female brains receive a measure of testosterone, but the female brain gets only small injections of the hormone while the male brain is flooded with it. And testosterone makes a huge difference. It stimulates strength, drive, and aggression, giving the average male a focus on power, competition, and winning. The low testosterone levels in the average female put her focus on nurturing, affection, sensitivity, and personal connections. The bulk of the man's communication is in pursuit of his competitive goals. The bulk of the woman's is in pursuit of relationships.

So in a sense, men and women live in two different worlds. When they marry and begin to build a shared world of their own, the two worlds they come out of can either collide or blend. More often than not, there's quite a bit of colliding before the blending begins as both sexes naively assume the other communicates in much the same way as they do. They are in for a huge surprise, not to mention inevitable misunderstandings that lead to conflict. Most of these conflicts come about because women tend to think men are insensitive and unfeeling, while men tend to think women are impossible to understand.

A man was riding along a California beach when suddenly a bright light broke through the clouds and a booming voice said, "This is the Lord speaking. Because you have been faithful to Me, I will grant you one wish."

The man pulled over and said, "I love Hawaii, but I hate to fly. Build me a bridge to Hawaii so I can drive over anytime I want."

"I can certainly do that," the Lord replied, "but think of the drain on natural resources—the supports required to reach the bottom of the Pacific, the millions of tons of concrete and steel. Don't you think it's a little selfish to ask all that just for yourself? Take a little more time and think of something more honorable."

The man thought for a while, and then he said, "Lord, I want to understand my wife. I want to know how she feels inside—what she's thinking, why she cries, what she really means when she says nothing's wrong, why she gives me the silent treatment—and how I can make her truly happy."

"Do you want that bridge two lanes or four?" replied the Lord.

All the jokes seem to be about men not understanding women, but in fact, it works both ways. The reason is that the innate differences between men and women result in different approaches and different ways of communicating. Therefore, each sex goes about the relationship in an altogether different way. Most men focus on the marriage as a thing to be built, maintained, and defended. He is the hunter/farmer. He goes out and applies his brain or brawn to wrest the needs of his home from a hostile world. When he comes home he's in his castle, his haven of rest, walled off and insulated from the threats and dangers he's fought all day. Most women focus on the marriage in terms of emotional connection. She, too, wants the home to be a protected haven, but for her it's one where intimate relationships can flourish. She finds her greatest security in an intimate connection with the heart of her husband.

Thus, for the most part, men and women have different needs, which they hope the marriage will satisfy. Men, the competitors, the mighty hunters, feel a need to be admired. Women, the nesters and nurturers, feel a need for emotional intimacy and security. They attempt to make this connection by communicating.

Both sexes communicate, of course, but the purpose and intent of their communication tends to differ, and they go about it in different ways. Men would like to reason their way into the relationship. They want to think through their moves and figure out why women act the way they do. If the woman, feeling a lack of emotional intimacy, expresses that need with tears, the man will often make the mistake of not moving toward empathy and understanding but rather toward analytical problem solving. He wants to fix whatever is wrong once and for all. The woman, on the other hand, often makes the mistake of believing that men's brains are wired exactly like women's—or should be. She expects him to want the same kind of emotional closeness that she does and to express it in intimate conversation. When things don't work that way, she often tries to remake him in order to meet those expectations.

Here's an example of a difference in the way men and women think. A handful of women meet at the tearoom of a suburban antique store. After they order, one says to the other,

"Oh, I love your new hairstyle. Who did it for you?"

"I decided to change stylists. This time I went to Madelyn's, and I'm just not sure if I like it. Do you think it's a little too short?"

"Oh, no, I just adore it! It makes your shoulders look great and shows off that elegant neck of yours. I'd die for your neck."

"But does it make my face look a little too wide?"

"No way. It brings out all your best features. It especially enhances your beautiful high cheekbones."

"I'm just so worried that Bill won't like it."

"Believe me, the moment he sees you he'll absolutely drool."

The truth is, Bill probably won't even notice his wife's new hairdo. Men, if you've been married any length of time you know how dangerous life can be when she comes home from the hairdresser. She'll sweep through the door all bright and smiling, waiting expectantly for your response. When it doesn't come, she'll say, "Well, what do you think?" still smiling.

"Um, what do I think about what?" You're clueless.

"Do you notice anything new?" Now you sense danger signals and feel panic. You do a quick inventory of her clothes and accessories. "Ah, yes. You got a new dress. It looks great."

"I've had this dress since last spring, and I've worn it a dozen times." Now her smile is gone and there's an edge in her voice. "Can't you see that I got a new hairdo? I thought you'd really like it, but you didn't even notice. After all I do to make myself attractive for you, you never look at me anymore."

"But I do like your hair. It looks great," you say, mustering up all the sincerity and enthusiasm you can. "It's just that you're so beautiful I have trouble tearing my eyes away from your face."

Too late. The damage is done. You see, in Bill's world, a world saturated with testosterone, hair would never be the subject of a serious conversation. If a man happens to notice a friend's new haircut at all, it's likely to provoke nothing more than a good-natured slam. "Man, what did your barber use on your hair, a hedge trimmer?" And far from being insulted, his friend will grin and return insult for insult, bonding more with each exchange. And then men will go on to rate each other's slams.

We should recognize up front that these responses are rooted in innate male and female differences, which were created for good purposes. Women want to be attractive; men want to be strong. Therefore while beauty is important to women, men want to appear competent and equal to their task. These differences between the sexes are meant to complement each other. Each supplies to the marriage what the other lacks. And when properly blended, the differences not only meet the varying needs of the marriage, but they become sources of real delight and mutual satisfaction. (Remember the exuberant French cry, "Viva le difference!")

When a wife criticizes her husband for not noticing

what all women would notice, she fails to accept him as he was created. And more often than not, when she succeeds in manipulating him into becoming more like her, she won't like the result. Women often feel disdain for men who under pressure compromise their masculinity and become feminized. They want and need their men to remain masculine, yet they long for more intimate communication.

We men don't need to become feminized, but we do need to move toward women in the area of communication and understanding. Talking to our wives will not make us less macho. Meeting a woman's needs is the epitome of masculinity. At the same time, women need to remember that men do not share their need to talk and understand that silence does not indicate a lack of love. Time, education, and insight can give a man more understanding of women, but to expect him to enter marriage with the same relational approaches as women is like wanting a dog to purr like a kitten.

By learning more of the nature and language of the other, each mate can achieve great communication in marriage. And, effective communication will double your marital satisfaction. That's a huge promise, but I've seen with my own eyes that it's absolutely true. Effective communication will make your marriage more intimate and peaceful and eliminate most of your escalated arguments. Expressing your feelings gives your mate a better understanding of your primary needs. The better you understand each other's primary needs—those mystifying mysteries that each of you brings from the masculine and feminine world—the deeper you can go into true intimacy.

While men and women come from different worlds, both need to be accepted, understood, and valued for who they are as God created them. Neither sex should selfishly expect to understand the other solely on one's own terms. Men need to be understood as men, and women need to be understood as women. That means work for both partners. We'll start with the men.

The Gaping Word Count Gap

Research tells us that women talk almost three times more than men. The average woman utters close to 25,000 words each day compared to the average man's 10,000. Women have a need to connect through words. Men simply don't have a need to talk as much. This difference contributes to many of the misunderstandings in every marriage. When the husband comes home in the evening, he's already spent his 10,000 words at work and has no energy left for communication. The wife, on the other hand, may be home with three children all day, and she is just warming up because she's got to get in her 25,000 words with an adult before sundown.

Now, men, here's where we need to move toward our wives. Ephesians 5 says that the husband is to love his wife as Christ loved the church, even to the point of dying for her. If you love your wife deeply enough to die for her, start by killing any of your own tendencies that harm her. This means start talking. She needs to talk. It's necessary to her happiness, her security, and even to her health. Whether you want to talk doesn't matter. If you love her you will want to meet her deepest needs. Start talking and make sure you are truly engaged in the process, not merely mouthing words from a sense of duty.[1]

As a man, what you say has more power than you think, affecting your wife and kids for the rest of their lives. God has given us men this mantle of power because we are the head of our family. If you withdraw into your own comfortable silence, the enemy is sure to fill the communication gap and talk to your wife. She will lie awake at night wanting so much to understand your heart that words will come into her mind to express what she thinks you are thinking. She may even believe you said things you never meant and get angry over things you never said, just because she was so starved for communication. She imagined the worst and it became her belief.

Increasing verbal communication is not as painful as men may think. Marriage expert, John Gottman, says a minimum of twenty minutes a day in true communication with each other decreases a couple's chances of divorce and greatly increases marital satisfaction. Just twenty minutes a day listening and talking with your mate, understanding each other's heart, and valuing each other's words. Who doesn't have at least that much time?

I know how we men are. When you come home in the evening, you've provided, so you've done your share. Your wife, however, still needs to spend her word allotment—especially if she's stayed at home all day—so she chatters all through dinner. To you the conversation may seem disjointed and unrelated to anything really important. It doesn't make more money. It doesn't provide anything. Dinner is over and she's still talking. You wonder why you're still sitting here. Now she wants to take coffee out to the front porch and continue the conversation. You want to head for the garage and fix that sputtering lawn mower.

Now stop and think, men. What's more important to you, the lawn mower? a hobby? cleaning the fishing pole for tomorrow's trip? or your wife? Remember, you'd die for her, right? Start by killing that urge to run away when conversation doesn't stop. You may have already spoken your 10,000 words, but there are plenty more in the dictionary. You're committed to growing older with this God-given, feminine creature who wants to sit and talk to you. Start cementing your relationship with communication today and your senior years together can be heavenly.

Besides building your relationship, a man's willingness to talk meaningfully with his wife provides many other proven benefits. The following are a mere sampling:

- Intimate talk increases a man's chances of staying healthy up to 500 percent.
- It reduces his chance of heart failure and all of the major illnesses.
- It increases the effectiveness of his immune system.
- It increases his wife's happiness and health.
- It increases his wife's sexual responsiveness to him.

Communication Is More than Just Talking

The mere fact that you open your mouth and a few words drift out doesn't necessarily mean you are communicating. Communication involves much more than just using words, and sometimes words do little to promote intimacy and understanding. Effective communication involves several actions at once—listening, speaking, facial expressions, tone of voice, and most of all, understanding. I want to discuss six levels of communication that are important to understand.

Level 1. Small talk or reflex words. The lowest level of intimacy is when you communicate with short clichés or reflex words that convey minimum information with minimum effort. "Pass the salt." "How's your day?" "Fine." "Okay." "Good." "Yeah right." "What did you do today?" "Nothing." "Oh." "Never." This kind of communication requires no concentration or effort. In terms of intimacy, it's almost meaningless.

This doesn't mean that small talk and reflex words are totally worthless. In comfortable marriages where the couples really know each other, the simple fact that amiable sounds are exchanged shows that the connection lines are open and no barriers exist between partners. Gottman says that such words can have more value if you turn to your mate and utter them with warmth and eye contact. This shows that you value your mate even when your words are few and mechanical.

Level 2. Communicating impersonal facts. This level of

communication is the simple, everyday exchange of external, nonpersonal information. "How's the weather out there?" "A little cold, but not too bad." "Can you believe what the president said today?" This level carries no intimacy, but it's friendly and safe. And there's a lot to be said for friendship communication. It seldom provides an occasion for an escalated argument.

Level 3. Sharing opinions. This third level of communication is the doorway to the most meaningful and satisfying levels. It involves expressing your opinions, concerns, and expectations. It can be like opening Pandora's box, however. All kinds of trouble can come from it. If your mate does not share your opinions, the warning light for potential conflict can start flashing. "I keep telling you that I hate it when we come here." "I never have liked this color for the kitchen." "When will you ever learn that I can't stand fried oysters?"

Statements like these can actually become doorways to deep levels of communication and intimacy. By applying just a little more communication skills, differences of opinion can move you to higher planes of understanding. Later in this chapter I'll show you how.

Level 4. Sharing deep feelings. The fourth level of communication is for mates to feel safe enough that they freely open up and reveal their deepest feelings to each other, knowing that what they reveal will be handled with love and care. Security is crucial at this level. Mates must feel utterly secure in each other's love before they will be willing to trust each other with their most intimate and vulnerable feelings. "I've been feeling a little lonely while you work on that church project." "Our decision to buy that house just doesn't feel right to me." "I know you love your class reunions, but somehow I feel left out."

Level 5. Sharing vital relational needs (physical, mental, spiritual, and emotional). This level of communication leads to the deepest experience of marital love and satisfaction. Understanding and responding to each other's deepest needs without judgment and recrimination demonstrates security and achieves oneness. "I really need your involvement with the children's discipline." "I need to feel wanted and cherished before I can respond sexually." "I need a half-hour alone to unwind when I get home in the evenings."

This level, of course, is difficult to reach. It means being open and honest with each other, and that means loving each other enough to allow honesty. Marriage partners often move into communication levels four and five through the doorway of conflict or disagreement. Disagreements are not negative; they occur when the masculine and feminine worlds come together, and they provide valuable inroads to intimacy. Properly communicated and resolved, disagreements between a couple help two people become one, because they enable each to see and respond to the other's viewpoint. Successful marriages put these last three levels at the core of all communication.

Level 6. Communicating your beliefs. The Bible tells us that above all else, we are to guard our heart. Since our heart contains our beliefs, sharing these beliefs with each other is the deepest level of communication. My wife and I spend hours talking about what we believe and where some of those beliefs came from. She was raised in an orderly and stable environment. Her dad came home on time every night for dinner. Her mother stayed home, ran the household, and cooked favorite meals for the family. She lived in the same house for over twenty years. Since her brother was out of the house before she was born, she was raised like an only child and became accustomed to being treated like a princess.

I, on the other hand, was the youngest of five children. My father changed jobs every year, and we moved almost as often. Being the baby of my family, I expected a lot of attention and had to have my needs instantly gratified.

As you can imagine, our marriage was a collision of worlds. And that collision generated a lot of heat and friction until we learned to communicate our deepest beliefs. Such beliefs, we realized, came from our backgrounds. Some of them needed to be changed. By communicating and exploring our different beliefs, we found out who we were and why we acted the way we did. Understanding each other's beliefs has greatly helped us to understand each other and to deal with our differences with love.

Hints for Heart-to-Heart Communication

Communication skills are not that complex or hard to learn. Many helpful books are out there, including a few of my own.[2] Here I'll give you just a few pointers to set you on the right track. Many of these involve listening as much as speaking, because listening is a key element in effective communication.

Use and read body language. Face your mate as you talk. If you are sitting, turn your chair toward him or her and relax. Unfold your arms and legs, as folded limbs send a subliminal message of being on guard or closed-minded. Unfolded limbs signal that you are letting down your guard and welcoming the other person inside your space.

As you talk, study your mate's body and face. Watch the facial expressions. Are the lips open? That indicates receptivity to what you're saying. Are they tightly closed? You are meeting resistance. Notice the hands and arms. If the hands are clenched or the arms are folded, your mate may be closed off to you. If they are relaxed, you are probably being heard. Sometimes these body signals can tell you things that words cannot. As you watch the body, ask the question, *What is she really saying? Is he on board with what I'm asking?* You might say, "I noticed that you looked away when I mentioned tightening our budget. What was on your mind? What is your opinion?" You want to get the most complete understanding you can. Learning to use and read facial expressions and body signals can do wonders for the process.

Use encouraging signals. Nods and acknowledging words let your mate know that you are listening actively. They demonstrate your focus on what the other is saying. It doesn't take much; a simple "Yes," "Uh-huh," or "I see," is usually adequate. Marriage experts have found that just making an affirming sound when the other is talking can increase marital satisfaction.

Restate your mate's core argument. Don't assume that you always understand the key points your mate is making. He or she may go on and on, and you may lose track of the real meaning. It's important that you hear what your mate is trying to tell you, so give a time-out signal to pause the conversation so you can verify your understanding: "Hold on a moment, let me repeat that back to see if I am getting it." Mates can avoid many misunderstandings and also be assured that the other is earnestly listening if each restates what they hear the other to be saying. "See if I'm hearing you right. You need some time alone at night after work. It's not that you don't want time with me, you just need a half hour to recoup?" "Are you saying you need more tenderness when we talk? Describe tenderness. What does it look like to you?" "Am I hearing this right, you want me to stop trying to fix you when you are upset? You just want me to listen? You're not looking for a solution, but you need me to understand your heart?" Your quest in all communication is to gain a more intimate understanding of each other. One step is to be sure you understand exactly what your mate is saying.

Make eye contact. This is often a particularly hard one for men during football season. But it's got to be done, guys. Eye-to-eye contact during conversation is almost as important as the words you say. If you listen to your mate's eyes, you will understand much better. Are his eyes looking straight at you? Then he's listening. Are her eyes looking away? She's not engaged in what you're saying. Is he squinting? He hears you but he's skeptical. Are her eyes wide open? She's drinking in every word. If you can learn to read the eyes, you will come to a much greater understanding of what your mate is really communicating and how he is responding to what you say.

One afternoon I was reading on the couch when my wife came in and said, "Something very important has come up that we need to discuss. I had a meeting with Terry this morning and—"

"Oh, I just realized it's five o'clock and time for my medicine," I interrupted as I jumped up and headed out of the room. "Come on in the kitchen and explain it while I'm mixing my medicine."

"No," she replied. "This is very important, and I want you looking at me, responding, concentrating, and not distracted."

"I'm just going into the kitchen. If you don't want to come, go ahead and talk. I can hear you from there." I didn't see any reason we couldn't do both things at once.

"No, I'm not saying a word until you come back in here and sit down."

So finally I drank my medicine, came back into the living room, sat down, looked at Norma, and only then did she begin speaking. She understood that effective communication means eye contact and full concentration on each other.

Set the scene. Eliminating distractions is paramount to effective listening. Turn off the TV, unplug the phone, and arrange for the kids to be out of your space. Let your mate know that talking, listening, and understanding each other is more important to you than anything else at that moment.

Communicating by Touch

Loving touches are the most powerful of all nonverbal communications. A marriage without touch is dry like a sponge deprived of water and leaves mates vulnerable to any drop of attention that comes their way. Consider the case of Kurt and Ginny.

Kurt had been distant from his wife their entire marriage. Ginny was like a dry sponge, longing for touches and hugs that Kurt never gave. One man where she worked sympathized with her when she was down and occasionally gave her an encouraging hug or a pat on the arm. His care was like a stream of water on Ginny's dry sponge, and she soaked it up.

Unknown to Ginny, Kurt had a friend in another department of the company where she worked. One day he told Kurt, "I've seen this guy at work hugging your wife. And she really seems to enjoy it."

Kurt was enraged. He confronted Ginny, and she admitted

the hugs and conversation but insisted that nothing more happened. It was too much for Kurt to swallow. He left her immediately and moved to an apartment in another town. Ginny was crushed, and she was barely able to get on with her life.

Eighteen months later Kurt had a massive heart attack. Doctors tried to stabilize him before performing a triple bypass, but they couldn't get control of his blood pressure. "Do you want us to notify your family?" they asked.

At first Kurt thought no, he would just die alone. But he relented and said, "Yes. Please notify my wife."

As soon as Ginny arrived the doctors warned her not to upset Kurt. "We are barely keeping him alive," they explained. She entered his room and gently touched his hand. He opened his eyes and tears began to flow.

"Honey, thank you so much for coming," he said. "I have missed you terribly all these months. I was so worried I'd never see you again." Ginny melted against him. For long moments nothing was said. Their entwined arms and bodies told the whole story. She began to choke out her confession but he interrupted.

"It's no wonder you wanted his touches after the way I starved your craving for love and affection. I've been so wrong. I realize now how distant and uncaring I was. I never touched you, never hugged you. But right now holding you means more to me than anything in the world. I want you in my arms, and I'm so sorry that I did this to you. If I could do it over again I'd lavish on you affection in words and touches every day to show you what a treasure you are to me. I'll never leave you parched again as long as I live. Will you please forgive me?" A tighter hug expressed her answer.

Immediately Kurt's heart stabilized, and within two weeks he was released. True to his word, he lavished love and affection on his treasured wife. And I've never seen a happier, more devoted couple.

We consistently underestimate it, undersell it, undervalue it, and underuse it. Yet touch has the power to calm, reassure, transfer courage, and stabilize a situation spinning out of control. When we touch our mates lovingly, we push back the threatening shadows of bitterness, loneliness, and insecurity. A loving touch can immediately drain anger from a situation. A gentle touch says, "You are valuable to me."

The proven power of touch is amazing. Medical studies show that men who meaningfully hug and touch others stay healthier and live longer. Research from Dr. Allan Shore, UCLA School of Medicine, shows that when babies aren't touched in their first two months, they can suffer permanent brain damage. Many children in understaffed orphanages die if they don't get touched. Would you like to lower your mate's blood pressure, improve your high school student's brain function, or protect your grade-school children from involvement in an immoral relationship later in life? Would you like to add up to two years to your own life? Findings in recent scientific studies show that touch can actually provide all these benefits. We give the people we care about an incredible gift when we reach out and touch them.

The UCLA studies found that to maintain emotional and physical health, men and women need eight to ten meaningful touches every day. (I mentioned this in a seminar once and noticed a man in the audience touching his wife several times on the shoulder as he counted to ten. That does not count as meaningful touch!) Touching on a regular basis triggers a chemical reaction in our brains that causes us to want more touching. This happens because touch stimulates the production of the hormone *oxytocin*. Oxytocin promotes a desire to touch and be touched: it's a feedback loop that multiplies what it generates. Oxytocin makes us feel good about the person who causes the oxytocin to be released, and it promotes bonding. Higher levels of oxytocin also result in greater sexual receptivity because oxytocin increases testosterone production, which is responsible for sex drive in both men and women.

Four Communication Germs that Can Kill Your Marriage

Does it seem that you can never have a discussion with your mate without arguing? If this is true of your marriage, you need to understand what may be burrowing beneath the surface that causes these outbreaks. Relationship experts have identified four main relational "germs" that can destroy marriage relationships. Let's look briefly at each of these insidious little bugs.

Withdrawal. Withdrawal occurs when one mate shuts out the other after an argument starts. Typical statements signaling withdrawal are: "End of discussion!" "I've said all I intend to say on this subject." "I'm not going to talk about this any more. It never does any good." or "This argument is over!" Withdrawal prevents resolution of differences and buries the germ under the surface where it can reemerge to infect the marriage again.

Escalation. Escalation occurs when mates become entrenched in their positions and focus on winning the argument instead of understanding each other. Signs of escalation are persistence in defending one's self and placing all the blame on the other person. Each mate fires volleys back and forth, shaming and blaming the other while defending their own actions. "How dare you blame me for being overdrawn. Do you really expect me to run this household on what you make?" "You think the kids watch too much TV because of *me?* Well, *you're* a great example!" Neither mate exhibits the humility of self-examination or forgiveness, and consequently their differences can never be resolved.

Belittling. When one mate accuses the other of being dumb or stupid, that is belittling. Usually a mate belittles to prove that he is better than the other—or at least has better judgment, opinions, understanding, or intelligence. This germ generates statements like, "That's the dumbest thing I've ever heard," or "Of all the stupid things you've done, this tops them all." Hardly the path to greater understanding!

Exaggerated or False Beliefs. One mate may believe that the other is intentionally doing things to weaken the marriage. Broad, global statements or false accusations are symptoms of this germ. "You always include your family in our private plans. They've come between us our whole married life!" "Obviously you don't really love me or you wouldn't always. . . ." Instead of engaging in real communication to search for the truth, one mate chooses to put the worst-case interpretation on the other's actions and play the blame game.

The way to kill these germs is through a communication method that resolves conflicts by truly seeking the best solution for both partners.

Win-Win Conflict Resolution

I'm closing this chapter by addressing one of the most important roles that communication can play in your marriage. According to Dr. Scott Stanley at Denver University, one of the best ways to overcome all four of the deadly germs within marriage is to learn the skills of conflict resolution. All husbands and wives have differing opinions about many things. Resolving these differences in the right way can bring you into a deeper, more loving relationship and increase your marital satisfaction by leaps and bounds.

Think of your mate as a picture puzzle. Each need, feeling, bit of communication, or belief is a piece. Your goal is to see how many pieces you can put together to complete the beautiful picture of that person God gave you to love and cherish. You fit the pieces together through open investigation, not by being critical and judgmental. This does not mean that when conflict arises you must simply roll over and give in. Communication is a two-way process. In a great marriage your needs and feelings will be as important to your mate as your mate's are to you. Both of you will keep the communication process going until you put the puzzle together, understanding each other's needs and finding ways to satisfy the two of you.

Good communication is crucial in the area of conflict resolution. I have assured you that when the masculine and feminine worlds meet, conflict is inevitable. But there is a way for both of you to come out winners. What may seem impossible can be resolved, as we will see in the story of Marty and Cheryl.

Marty was reading his mail after dinner when his wife Cheryl came in and sat beside him. In her hand was a clipping from a magazine showing a beautiful couple on a romantic beach, running from the surf to their beach blanket and umbrella.

"Honey, look what I found," she said. "Wouldn't the beach be a great vacation this July? We could drive there in little over a day. Imagine, just the two of us, enjoying the sun, the surf, great food, dancing, snuggling, and shows in the evening."

Marty looked at the ad for a moment without replying.

He knew Cheryl loved romantic getaways where just the two of them could be totally wrapped up in each other. But they had done this recently, and he had other ideas. "Well, honey," he said. "That looks great, but I sort of had my heart set on spending a few days at a NASCAR track. We went to the beach last year, you know."

To say that Cheryl cared nothing for NASCAR events was an understatement. She thought her ears would never stop ringing from the last time she went. But she knew her husband loved NASCAR and seldom had a chance to see it, as there was no track near their city. "Well, maybe we could take two vacations," she said. "We can go to the beach in June and to the racetrack at Bristol in August."

"I don't think so, Cheryl. Two trips would be pretty expensive for us right now. You know how tight our budget is after having to replace our air conditioner."

"It's a little tight because it includes savings," she replied. "And that's a good thing. But as hard as we work, we need time away. We need to get in touch with each other. I think the money would be well spent."

"I don't think we're out of touch," replied Marty. "We both get busy, but we have each other, and that makes all the difference. Why not just get away for a weekend in the city? We could stay a couple of nights at a hotel, see a play, and drive back before Monday."

"That's just not the same," said Cheryl. "It takes more than a weekend to really unwind and reconnect."

Marty didn't feel the need like Cheryl did, but he understood that she was expressing the belief she felt in her heart. She felt that they were getting a little disconnected, and she was convinced that a couple of weeks to themselves would do wonders.

"OK, see what you think of this," he said. "Hotels give great discounts in September just after the peak tourist season. There's a big NASCAR event in Atlanta in mid-September. See what kind of hotel deal you can get in Florida just after that. We could drive to Atlanta in one day, spend three days at the track, then drive on down to the beach and spend the rest of our vacation there."

"Oh, that sounds great!" Cheryl replied, throwing her arms around her husband and kissing him warmly. "I'll get on the Internet right now." An hour later she returned with a package deal that was half the price of the one in the magazine clipping. Marty loved it, and they made reservations that very night.

Marty and Cheryl came into their vacation discussion with different needs. It's not uncommon in such disagreements for couples to ignore the needs of each other, to focus only on their own, and try to browbeat the other into compliance. Instead of listening to understand his wife, Marty could have thought, *There she goes, wanting to spend money again. Does she think I'm made of gold? Why does she always insist on going to a romantic beach? Does she think every vacation has to be to some girly place? It's time I got the vacation I want for a change!*

Marty and Cheryl didn't let their differences get in the way of their love. Each looked into the heart of the other without judgment or condemnation and made an effort to understand. Marty didn't want what his wife wanted, but he loved her enough to want her needs met. He listened to her through the filter of his love. He didn't jump to the conclusion that her desire for a beach vacation was just a selfish disregard of his own preferences. Instead, he listened for the belief behind her desire and saw her need for deeper connection.

Dr. Scott Stanley says that a major factor in a happy marriage is learning to negotiate differences. The most common differences occur in the areas of money, sex, in-laws, and children. But they can occur over absolutely anything. I remember a difference Norma and I had over a moose head, of all things. I found this beautiful moose head that fit perfectly in the living area of our guest lodge. When Norma saw it, she was horrified and insisted that I take it down. I wanted it to stay because it was appropriate for our décor. She wanted it out of there because it was "the ugliest thing" she'd ever seen. She suggested I hang it in the garage. That didn't work for me. After a round or two of negotiation, we finally agreed to hang it in the guest bedroom. She was happy—it was out of sight to most visitors—and I was happy—it would stay in the lodge. We came to a win-win solution.

I want to do a lot of things, but I can't just do whatever I want because I'm married to a person who has beliefs, needs, and feelings of her own. We love each other and neither wants the other to feel trampled on. So we operate by this rule: When we disagree, we don't move forward until both of us feel good about the solution. Now, as a guy living in the competitive masculine world, I don't like to lose. But when my wife says to me, "I don't want to move forward until you're happy," I relax. She doesn't want me to lose. And because I love my wife, I don't want her to lose either.

Marty and Cheryl, and Norma and I, followed three basic steps to a win-win solution to our differences.

1. We communicated honestly without judgment of the other. We listened to the other's feelings, needs, and beliefs, and openly communicated our own. We didn't try to change our mates or pressure them to yield to our own preferences. We listened for the heart beneath the words.
2. We placed on the table ideas and alternatives, discussing their pros and cons and testing each for acceptability to the other.
3. We found solutions that both partners liked.

Solutions like these do more than just resolve a difference; they show enormous honor between mates and increase security in the marriage. When the Bible tells us that husbands and wives become "one flesh," the term in the original means "blended." The masculine and feminine worlds come together like two liquids, each a different color, being poured together. The result is not two separate colors sharing space side-by-side in the container, but a total blending that creates an altogether new color. The masculine and feminine are blended into a new kind of thing that's different from either. That kind of harmonious blending is what takes place when mates love each other enough to seek win-win solutions to their conflicts.

Making the Promise

I hope I've helped you see how crucial good communication is to your marriage relationship. I strongly encourage you to promise your mate that you will always listen to his or her deepest needs, feelings, and beliefs, and that you will openly communicate your own. Promise that you will honor the opinions and beliefs of each other. Promise to listen without judgment or condemnation, with an intent to honor every thought your mate expresses. This promise will create and maintain an atmosphere of safety and security in your marriage, where neither of you will fear to speak openly with the other.

Promise that when your needs, feelings, or beliefs differ, you will seek a solution that works for both of you. Promise that when you disagree, you will not go forward until both of you feel good about the solution. Such a promise will create an oneness between the two of you that is greater than all your masculine and feminine differences. It will turn those differences into strengths that will enhance your marriage and delight both of you all the days of your life together.

Coming Up Next...

In the final chapter, I'll show you how to make a promise that is possible only if God is your strength, hiding His words like Matthew 22:37–40 and Galatians 5:13 in your heart. This last promise is of great importance to God. When you make it and fulfill it, you put yourself right in the center of His eternal will for you.

CHAPTER 8

I Promise to Serve You All the Days of My Life

*R*ecently I had an insight that I probably should have thought of long ago. I was out of town and decided to walk two miles along a quiet road. Before long, a beautiful, well-formed girl wearing the briefest of shorts and skimpiest of halters came jogging by. After she passed I asked myself: *Why do I, at age sixty-five, still have lustful thoughts? When will I stop being tempted as if I were still sixteen?* It occurred to me that if all my feelings and actions come from the beliefs in my heart, maybe I have an old belief from childhood stuck in there that's driving these thoughts. I didn't know what that belief was, but I knew that if I lacked wisdom, I could ask God. We can talk to Him about anything without feeling embarrassed. As David acknowledged in Psalm 139, the Lord already knows everything about me. So why not bring my beliefs about lust before Him so He can show me how to deal with them?

Within minutes, it hit me. I was raised in an environment in which my father and older siblings seemed totally focused on seeking pleasure for themselves, regardless of the feelings or needs of others around them. Most of their attention was on things like fishing, hunting, movies, food, dating, sex, affairs, gambling, vacations, water sports, skiing, or anything that would bring about the greatest amount of pleasure. So I grew up with the basic belief instilled in me that life is for pleasure and gratification. Without me really being aware of it, I developed a huge portion of my heart to seek pleasure.

As I walked that day, I began to remember Scriptures that teach the very opposite. The one that stood out was Galatians 5:13:

"For you have been called to live in freedom—not freedom to satisfy your sinful nature, but freedom to serve one another in love."

My freedom in Christ was not given to enable me to pursue sexual or exciting pleasures, but rather to serve others by loving them in the same way that I would like to be loved. The focus of my life is not to be on me and my own gratification, but on the good of others. Instead of serving myself, I get to serve others.

Now, the idea of serving others was not new to me. As you will see in this chapter, early in my marriage I learned the importance of serving my wife, and later the importance of serving others. But one of the exciting things about the Christian life is that new things keep unfolding—even about what you already know. It never occurred to me until I went walking that day that committing myself to unselfish service to others could change even an old habit like lust. Once we adopt the attitude that we are here to serve, just as Christ was, all areas of our lives are changed for the better.

As I continued to walk, I repeated Galatians 5:13 over and over, working the principle of service into my heart to replace the selfishness of lustful thoughts. Day after day, I began to think more about serving others through love than about using some female for my pleasure. As I focus on changing my beliefs by hiding God's Word in my heart, I'm always amazed at how fast my actions change naturally. Within two weeks of memorizing this verse and repeating it back to God from morning till night, lustful thoughts began to disappear. Now when a lustful thought moves toward me, I simply say to God, "I used to be a hedonist Lord, but You have given me the power to serve others through Your love." Now instead of fantasizing when I see a beautiful girl, I wonder if she knows how much God loves her. Does she have a father or husband who loves her? I hope that she will someday discover God's best for her life. I tell God that I can't wait to share this with men all over the world who truly want God's best.

The idea of serving others instead of using people never entered my head when I first married Norma. Using her became my natural habit; I didn't even think about it. I just expected her to serve me like Dad and the whole family expected my mom to serve us. If I came home hungry after a date, Mom would jump out of bed and make me a butterscotch pie. (As you might imagine, Norma drew the line at this request.) My problem was that I believed a wife's role was to serve her husband. I had Ephesians 5:24 down pat: "As the church submits to Christ, so you wives must submit to your husbands in everything." This verse made everything clear: I was the leader and she was the servant. Of course I somehow managed not to notice the rest of Paul's admonitions in this chapter.

In the first year of our marriage I was a youth pastor, and I had volunteered to be on the church basketball team. I often neglected to tell Norma when games were scheduled, so I called her from the church office one day to inform her of a game that night.

"Hey Norm," I said. "I have a game tonight, and you know I always like you to be there to watch. Afterward, we can eat out." There was a long silence, and though we hadn't been married long, I knew already that long silences didn't bode well. "So that's a good plan, right?" I said.

"Gary, today is Valentine's Day," Norma finally answered with a quiver in her voice. "I have already begun cooking a special dinner for us. Couldn't you skip this one game so we can have our first Valentine's dinner together?"

How had I failed to see Valentine's Day coming with all the red signs in stores and all the shelves filled with candy, cards, and balloons? As I thought about it, I vaguely remembered her mentioning this dinner about two weeks before. I had forgotten. But I had a solution: "Okay, come on to the gym and we can heat up the meat after the game? How does that sound?"

Pause, and more pause. She was thinking, *Does he think a*

stupid basketball game on a team that hasn't won all year is more important than our very first special candlelight Valentine's dinner together? Finally, unable to talk because of her tears, Norma whispered, "Gary, if you want to play, you go right ahead. I'll stay home and keep cooking, and we'll eat when you get here."

How warm do you think the dinner was when I got home? You guessed it. The food was lukewarm, and the wife was arctic cold. No snuggling that night. Her spirit was scraping bottom because she saw that my priorities were always what made me feel good—fun and games, church stuff, fishing— and then somewhere down the line, her. I was serving mainly my own needs. Her feelings and needs hardly registered. I was not a servant to my wife.

The "aha" experience for me—which started my entire ministry with marriage and family—happened five years later over a lunch break. I was pastoring my first church, and I was so committed to ministering that I even told Norma that God was first, my ministry was second, and she was third. At first she went along with that. She was young. The only problem was that it didn't work. God was not happy with me putting my ministry over my wife, and it didn't take long for her to feel the same way. As the kids came along, she felt more and more isolated from me. I lived in two different worlds, and my actions made it clear that my real world was my ministry. My home was merely a pit stop. My church, my youth group, my committees, preaching, and teaching were more important to me because they got me praise and appreciation. Norma tried to talk to me about all this, and I probably said something like,

"Okay, I'll try to do better," but I didn't really hear her.

How well I remember the day everything came crashing down. It was a hectic time at the church, but I decided to go home and have lunch with Norma. I bounded enthusiastically into the kitchen, and said, "Hey, what's for lunch?" When I tried to hug her, she bristled and wouldn't turn around.

"What's wrong?" I asked.

"Nothing you want to hear." She stood at the sink, cold and distant as death. I sat down, still wanting to eat, but nothing was prepared.

"Come on, tell me what's wrong?" I repeated two or three times.

Finally she responded. "What's the point? It never does any good. All you do is talk, but nothing ever changes. Everything else in your life is more important than I am. Your fishing, every kid you work with, everybody in church, every committee, the basketball team, the church building, even the television, are all more important to you than I am. You come home and act like I don't even exist. You plop down and watch television or read the paper. Then you eat dinner, go off to some meeting or appointment, and never even thank me.

"Somebody will call during dinner and you'll say, 'No, I'm not doing anything important,' and off you go. '*I'm not doing anything important*.' Can't you see how it cuts me deep inside to hear you say that when you're with your wife and children? We're not important? I feel like your prostitute, your housekeeper, your children's nanny, while the church is your mistress. I really don't even want to live with you anymore. I'm resolved to stay in the marriage out of obedience to God, but I'm dead inside toward you. There isn't a marriage here, and my heart is gone."

I was utterly stunned. Yes, she had been on my case about spending more time with her, but I had no idea it had come to this. Her words cut me to the core. I had been in India where some women are treated no better than dogs. They have no money, no rights, and they are beaten every day. Many women don't meet their husband until the day of the wedding. Parents must pay their daughter's future husband a sizeable sum of money, which is determined by his family lineage and his position in the community. When a girl's family has no money, she often grows past the ideal age for marriage with no suitors. When she realizes she's not likely to ever marry, she kills herself by jumping off a bridge. The suicide rate among women in India is astronomical. Naturally, I was appalled at this terrible treatment of women and thought the whole system needed a radical overhaul. How easy it was for me to judge another country's culture while being blind to my own situation! I was treating Norma almost as poorly.

I had a log in my eye, and it was selfishness, an ugly thing with knots and twisted branches of immaturity and ego. I placed myself at the center of the universe and expected others to orbit around me. I had the "I want to be God" attitude. I wanted to be worshiped, admired, adored, and blessed by others. That attitude drew my attention outside my home to my church, where I found admirers ready to lay lavish accolades on me for my great work in the kingdom.

I could see that our marriage was in big trouble, and the future looked almost hopeless. She had given up on the relationship. She was dead to me. I saw no handle I could grasp to pull our relationship back from the edge. Maybe it was the gravity of the situation that gave me clarity in that moment. Somehow, I didn't need hours of self-examination to filter out the truth. It hit me in a flash that she was dead on 100 percent accurate. I had been wrong not to make her my priority. I had been wrong to place serving the church above serving her.

"You are right," I said to Norma. "I admit it. I've made everything else in my life more important than you. Even fishing is more important to me than you. I am so ashamed. I promise right now that I will put you first in my life. You will be my number one priority, above friends, fishing, counseling, and even above the church. I may lose my job over it, but that's okay. I would rather lose my job than you. I beg you to forgive me. If you can't do it yet, I understand. Things didn't get in this shape overnight, and you may not believe I can really change."

That day I promised her that she would be my top priority over everything else on earth. But on my way back to work, a dark cloud descended on me as I realized that my life was now over. No more fishing, working late, golfing, weekends with friends—I was dead. I wanted to call her back when I returned to work and say, "I didn't really mean I would put you above *everything* else, just most things."

But by the power of God, I did change. Every morning I got up looking for ways to serve my wife—to put her first over everything else. From that time on, I was always home at night. If someone called with a ministry request that would take me away, I said, "Sorry, I can't do that tonight. I'm with my wife and family." Norma heard those answers and, in time, they began to soften her attitude toward me.

One night, after a few months of regularly being home in the evenings with my family, the phone rang just after dinner. Norma took the call, and after a moment she put her hand over the receiver and said, "The Smiths need help desperately. They are about to separate tonight. They want you to come over right now."

"No way," I said. "I want to spend the evening with you."

"I appreciate that so much," she replied, "but it sounds like they really, really need somebody now. I would gladly give up this evening with you if you could help them."

"No, you are my priority. I want to stay here."

"Please go help them," she said graciously. "They really seem to need it."

"All right," I said, "But only if you bless this time."

She blessed it, just as she has done many times since. Just think of all the ministry opportunities that have been born out of my change in priorities. That day I came home started a whole new life for both of us. I broke through the barrier of self-centeredness and began developing new beliefs about serving others instead of using others. I changed my heart's beliefs about my role as a husband. I began to understand what an older mentor of mine had tried to tell me: "Ministry to others comes from how you are ministering first at home."

I know that serving in a marriage applies equally to both husbands and wives, but it's so easy for us men to distort what the Bible teaches as an excuse to misuse women. We point to passages about wives submitting to husbands and ignore those about husbands serving wives. Yes, submission is part of a marriage, but husbands forget God asks this of husbands as well. A few paragraphs earlier I told you how I focused on Ephesians 5:24, where Paul tells wives to submit to their husbands. Somehow I managed to ignore the rest of that chapter where Paul lays upon husbands a huge responsibility toward their wives. Look at some of his words: "Husbands ought to love their wives as they love their own bodies. . . . No one hates his own body but lovingly cares for it." "Each man must love his wife as he loves himself." And most important: "And you husbands must love your wives with the same love Christ showed the church. He gave up His life for her to make her holy and clean. . . ."

After reading these Scriptures, men who think women were created to be their servants, sex objects, and flunkies should think again. Actually, it comes nearer to being the other way around. The Bible seems to give men the greater responsibility toward serving and caring for our wives. They serve us to the point of submitting, but we serve them to the point of dying. Think of it in terms of what it takes to put breakfast before you in the mornings. The ham on your plate requires a greater sacrifice than the eggs. The chicken submits an egg, but the pig lays down its life. That's the kind of sacrifice men must be willing to make for their wives. Our service to them is not lesser than theirs to us—it's greater.

Our Great Servant Mentor

The way I treated Norma might have been different had there been people in my life to demonstrate servant living. Far from being a servant, my father was out for himself only. When we fished together he would kick me out of his favorite fishing spots. No one at seminary trained us budding pastors in the fine art of serving our wives, and this is a huge gap in the education of ministers. My mentor in the ministry was a pastor who proudly showed me his monthly calendar with every day, but one, crammed morning through evening with church work. This man lost his wife because he was never home. Not one of my Christian educators or mentors ever addressed the need to spend time with one's wife or serve her in any way. So the idea never occurred to me.

But when the scales fell off my eyes, I found that I had the ultimate Mentor right before me all along—Jesus Christ Himself. Jesus gave us the best possible example of living the life of a servant. As He told His disciples, "For even I, the Son of Man, came here not to be served but to serve others, and to give my life as a ransom for many" (Matthew 20:28). In Philippians 2:1–11, the apostle Paul urges us to serve as Christ did, outlining six areas characteristic of a true servant:

1. Purpose: Be united with Christ in purpose: with his spirit, love, compassion, and tenderness (vv.1–2).

2. Motive: Get rid of selfish ambition (v. 3). Become "other-focused."

3. Attitude: Humility (v. 8). God gives grace to the humble and opposes the proud (James 4:6).

4. Action: Consider others more important than yourself (vv.3–4). The greatest commandment is to love God and to love others as you love yourself (Matthew 22:37–39).

5. Position: Jesus took the lowest role (v. 7). He was a servant with a small "s." The word doulos, or bond-servant, means slave by choice. A doulos slave was set free and then willingly chose to remain in service to his master.

6. Sacrifice: Jesus was obedient to serve God to the point of dying for all mankind (v. 8). That is the ultimate example of servanthood.

Jesus is the perfect mentor for developing a life that serves our mate and others. He is the Lord of the universe, but He showed in His earthly life that the highest calling of a great leader is to be a servant. Luke 22:24 shows us the human struggle that we all have experienced. Jesus' disciples were caught up in their own ambition for success and power, arguing over who would be the greatest in the coming kingdom. But Jesus rebuked them saying, "Those who are the greatest should take the lowest rank, and the leader should be like a servant. Normally the master sits at the table and is served by his servants. But not here! For I am your servant."

Jesus was telling them that true leadership is not insisting on being the one in charge, making all the decisions, and determined to rule the roost. A true leader looks to the needs of others and sees that they are met. The real reason we elect all our leaders—mayors, governors, presidents—is so that they can serve people and make lives as equitable and profitable as possible. But aspiring leaders often forget the servant nature of leadership and seek office for power and prestige. We husbands must avoid that trap. When I grow up I want to be a leader like my big brother Jesus. I want to be known as a servant.

What do you look like when you become like Jesus? The picture that always comes to my mind is the image of Him wearing a towel, bending over the dirty feet of those twelve dear friends, washing away the grime of the road. We become most like Christ when we serve others.

Being a servant in marriage is putting your mate first—even above yourself—and giving yourself for the other. For Christ this meant dying for others, and in some rare cases, it may mean that in a marriage. But love seldom requires a once-and-for-all sacrifice of life or limb. Usually the giving of yourself is an ongoing thing, a continuing attitude that looks perpetually to the welfare of your mate. It's saying, "I promise to make you more important than me. I promise to put your needs above my own. I promise to give up my preferences and even my needs if it serves your well-being."

How can laying aside your own wants and serving others

possibly make you happy? Well, the only way to understand it may be to try it. I can assure you that my happiest times have always been those in which I was clearly adopting the attitude of a servant. I'm not being a servant if I expect anything in return—even appreciation. Those desires for ego affirmation or reciprocation are logs that need to be rooted out. Jesus never asked for anything back. His service to us was all about giving. He said, "I'm going to give My life so that you might have life." If I am like Christ, I will want to give my life to my mate so that she will have life.

I love what my pastor, Ted Cunningham, says about his marriage: "I can trace all of my conflicts with my wife to my lack of serving her or not understanding her deeply enough. When I die to myself and take the time to really listen and understand what she needs, I not only stay in harmony with her, but our relationship is great on all levels."

If you want a happy marriage, the best way to get there is to not make a happy marriage your ultimate goal, but simply to become more like Christ. Jesus was a servant, and He said that the greatest people are those who choose to be servants like He was. Serve your mate selflessly, and you will find happiness in marriage. That's why my goal in marriage is no longer to be a great husband; it's to be a great servant. Great servants make great marriages.

Free Yourself for Service

A primary characteristic of a servant is a willingness to yield one's own rights. What do we mean by rights? We all have basic needs. In addition to those needs we also have basic wants—things not absolutely necessary but highly desired in order to maintain a certain level of quality in our lives. Those wants quickly tend to turn into needs, and from needs they morph into rights that we believe we deserve—the right to comfort, protection, fairness, opinions, recreation, down time, and so on. Rights can get very detailed, down to our right to eat certain foods, to behave in certain ways, or to live our chosen lifestyle. In short, we begin to think we have the right to pursue whatever pleases us. You can see how this attitude interferes with the posture of a servant. Demanding our rights eclipses the needs of others.

Modeling our lives after Jesus turns the idea of rights on its head. As Paul puts it, "I have been crucified with Christ. I myself no longer live, but Christ lives in me. So I live my life in this earthly body by trusting in the Son of God, who loved me and gave himself for me" (Galatians 2:19b–20). We no longer live for our rights and pleasures. We put them to death and now live for Christ. We give them up to God and live by faith that He will take care of all our needs. Remember, as I said in chapter 4, since God meets all of my needs, I am freed to concentrate on meeting the needs of others.

The old hymn "I Surrender All" expresses the idea very well. Each time I have surrendered all to God, He has used me in ministering to others far more effectively than when I was still pursuing my rights. We tend not to notice the needs of others when we are preoccupied with our own pleasure. Giving up your rights is the key to laying down your life for your mate. Instead of being on the take for self, genuine serving delights in giving. Genuine serving says, "I'll serve you because God is changing me into the image of His Son, and His Son is a servant." This kind of serving gives God control over your future, which frees you from focusing on yourself so you can serve others.

Becoming a Genuine Servant to Your Mate

Do you really know your mate? Have you managed to put aside your own rights so you can focus on what makes your husband or wife tick? Have you made it your goal to study your mate to know the innermost desires and needs in his or her heart? To be a servant in marriage you must know your spouse. Genuine serving means learning to identify your husband's or wife's specific needs and looking for creative ways to meet them.

I stress the need for each to learn the other's needs, because it's all too easy to assume that your mate's needs are the same as your own. When this happens you may plunge in all gung-ho with good intentions of serving, yet fail to meet the true needs of your mate's heart. Our normal habit is to see things from our own perspective with little understanding of the viewpoint of others. To be a genuine servant, you must know your mate's heart.

Anna and Mike came to me for counseling. Anna claimed that her husband made her feel unloved. Mike was dumbfounded and frustrated by this claim.

"I do everything, but stand on my head to please her," he said. "And I'll even do that if it will help. I can't imagine what more she could possibly want."

I asked Anna to explain what she meant.

"Well, he has been a great husband and a very helpful person, and he does lots of nice things for me. I know it sounds ungrateful to say it, but . . . well . . . he's always doing things I don't need. He gives me advice when I need comfort. He's great with flowers for every occasion, but not so great with loving words. He's great with sex, but not with hugs and touches any other time. He shares the household chores, but not his innermost feelings. He serves me in ways that seem important to him, but I would love it if he would find out what's important to me."

Mike's face went red with embarrassment. And I understood why. Been there, done that. The average husband has no clue about what's really important to his wife. We're dimly aware that women want security, so we believe we're serving them by providing and protecting. We often fail to see that security means much more to them than solid walls, a steady income, and a stocked pantry. They want security, not only from outside danger and want, but security in the relationship.

OK, guys. Our testosterone-soaked minds are not likely

to pick this up intuitively. We need a list of our wives' needs that we can analyze and check off. Very well, here it is. I keep this list in my desk. It contains ten things I've learned over the years concerning my wife's real needs. I consult it every week to assess how I'm doing in serving her. Sometimes I pass with flying colors; sometimes I rate a C-minus. But I do a lot better with the list than I would if I just flew by the seat of my pants. By the way, wives, this list will also work for you in helping you to love your husband more.

1. My spouse needs to feel valued—more valuable to me than my children, my job, my friends, or my hobbies.
2. My spouse needs open and unobstructed communication. If this has not been my habit, then work on it a little at a time.
3. My spouse needs my shoulder before my mouth. Empathy and comfort should precede advice or a solution to the problem.
4. My spouse needs to know I will defend and support her or him. If what my spouse is doing is indefensible and insupportable, then I should support the potential to change.
5. My spouse needs to be held and touched. God made us to connect, and meaningful touch is incredibly powerful.
6. My spouse needs to be praised verbally. Praise shows I notice and appreciate what my mate does. The lack of praise conveys little worth.

7. My spouse needs help. The best help is without commentary on how the other does things. If I am unsure how to help, ask for direction.
8. My spouse needs to share our lives together in every area. This moves us toward oneness.
9. My spouse needs support when life is falling apart. Support is not lectures and advice. The essence of support is a caring attitude.
10. My spouse needs my prayers, spiritual focus, and transparency about my walk with God. My relationship with Christ should not be held private from my mate.

This list works for me, and it may work for you as a starter. But I suggest that you tailor your list to fit your mate's specific needs and not depend permanently on mine. Remember, part of serving is getting inside your mate's heart, so that you know his or her needs, feelings, beliefs, interests, or tastes intimately.

How do you discover what your mate's needs are? Well, you might consider just asking. Sometimes we make things more complex than they need to be. If you want information, asking and listening are often the simplest and most effective ways to get it.

When Norma and I were about to move our family from Waco to Phoenix, we knew the relocation would be hard on our kids. So after dinner each night, we remained around the table and encouraged them to share their concerns and needs. We found that our youngest son, Michael, feared finding new friends. Greg was afraid he would not make the baseball team in a larger school. Each family member shared from the heart, and we made a list of what all of us would like to see happen in the move so that one year later each of us could say, "This was my best year ever."

The family readjustment went beautifully. It was the most successful team-building project we had ever tried. Each of us thought of different ways to make each other's dreams come true. It was so effective for our family that Norma and I started practicing the same technique in our relationship. We questioned each other about our hopes and needs, and then followed up every few months to check our progress. Becoming a genuine servant in marriage simply means getting inside the heart of your mate.

If you need help getting inside your mate's heart, there is no shortage of books on the subject, including many I have written myself, such as *The DNA of Relationships*. Other excellent guides are Gary Chapman's *The Five Love Languages* and Willard F. Harley's *His Needs, Her Needs*. These are fine books for helping you learn relational skills, but let me remind you that none of these skills will be 100 percent effective unless your mate feels secure and safe with you. Serving is a powerful method of securing safety in your marriage.

How My Job Helped Me Become a Better Servant at Home

I told you earlier how I learned to put Norma first in my life and began to serve her. I guess I'm a slow learner, because that lesson of service didn't automatically take in other areas of my life. I had to flunk before the lesson sank in.

When I was still the assistant pastor at a large church, I worked under a strong but loving senior pastor. I hadn't been there long before I was put in charge of the church's educational program. I was always full of ideas and needs for my ministries, which I placed before the board at every meeting. But my proposals were almost always voted down. I became terribly frustrated because I seldom got anything approved. Finally I had had enough.

I slithered home and complained to Norma about how uncaring and shortsighted these church leaders were. I was going to quit. She encouraged me to do a little self-examination. Find at least one thing I might be doing that would cause the church to react so negatively to my ideas. I was a little peeved that she would suggest the possibility that it could be, even a smidgen, my fault. But I told her that I would not eat or sleep again until God showed me one thing I was doing to contribute to the conflicts I was having at the church.

That night I prayed, read the Bible, drank water, prayed, read, and prayed some more, but nothing happened. I couldn't think of one thing that might be my fault. Then I started reading Galatians 5, and when I hit verse 13, it hit me back. "For you have been called to live in freedom—not freedom to satisfy your sinful nature, but freedom to serve one another in love." I had begun to learn to serve Norma, but had I learned to serve my bosses at the church? No. I was not serving them;

I was serving my own vision. I had been trained at a university, a seminary, attended numerous youth leadership conferences, been mentored by other pastors, and I was heading a church education department and youth ministry. I had all the credentials, and I had arrived. Why didn't everyone just listen to my expertise and give me what I needed to do my job? I was a trained professional, for heaven's sake!

There was the problem, staring me in the face. I was utterly self-focused, and that kept me from "serving one another in love." I wanted the staff to serve *my* dreams for the church. I wanted them to help *me* become successful with *my* goals. But I didn't have a clue as to the goals of the senior pastor or the church leadership, much less what the parents wanted for their kids. I wasn't serving them at all. I wanted the whole church to serve me and help me become youth pastor of the year.

Confronting my failure to serve made me sick inside. I didn't go to bed, but stayed up and prayed the rest of the night. And as soon as the pastor arrived the next morning, I asked to see him. He probably thought I was about to resign, because he knew I was very frustrated. I sat across the desk from him, and the first words out of my mouth were, "Pastor, could you forgive me for using you and the church to meet my goals? I don't even know where God is leading you with this church. I've never bothered to find out. I hope you can forgive me for my selfishness and failure to be a servant to you and this church. If you will share your goals with me, I promise to start using what skill and ability I have to help you meet them."

The pastor stood up, came around the desk, hugged me and forgave me. Then he spent three hours sharing all of his dreams, frustrations, discouragements, and hopes for the church. From that moment on, I pitched in and did all I could to help him meet his goals. It was a huge turnaround for our relationship. I became like a son to him, and his mentoring blessed my life more than I can ever say. With that experience, God broadened my understanding of what it means to be a genuine servant.

What do you think happened the next time I brought up my ideas for helping the church move forward? The board and the pastor approved everything, because my ideas were really their ideas wrapped in my creative methods. I simply used my own skills and know-how to serve their goals.

What Goes Around Comes Around

I've been careful to say that genuine service is never motivated by what you can get in return. There is, however, often a direct and visible return, which can bless your life enormously. As my final illustration, I'll relate to you a personal experience showing how God blessed my life when I became serious about learning to serve.

As I began serving Norma, she became more relaxed and secure in our marriage. This enabled her to begin looking into my heart to see my dreams. I remember the day in Waco, Texas, when she looked into my eyes and said,

"Gary, it's time for you to strike out on your own. It's great that you've given your life to so many people and ministries, but now you should begin doing what God has called you to do."

"What is that?" I asked.

"You need to be doing what you do best—save marriages, strengthen relationships."

"I'm not sure I can do it on my own," I replied.

"We can do it together. I can see into your heart, Gary. This is your dream; it's your talent, and it's what God wants you to do. I'll be there to help you every step of the way. It's time to get your dream off the ground. I believe in you, Gary. You tell me what dreams God is placing in your heart, and I'll be your dream maker."

That did it for me. With encouragement like that, I felt I could leap tall buildings with a single bound. So we plunged in. Once I let people know what I was about, support of all kinds came from all directions. Every member of the church staff gave me enormous encouragement. They even adopted my new ministry as a missionary effort and supported me financially. Baylor University students went home and told their pastors about me, and soon churches all over America began calling me to conduct marriage seminars. From there, my ministry grew beyond my wildest dreams.

It could never have happened without Norma listening to my dreams and helping bring them to reality. She has been a godsend to me. With her superb gifts of organization and attention to detail, she has managed my ministry for over forty years. Now I trust her so much that I often don't even know where I'm heading to share the message God has given me. I just grab the tickets and itinerary on the way out the door and figure it all out when I get on the plane. I never need to know how much money we have or how the staff is doing. She takes care of everything. I couldn't have designed a woman who would be a better match for me. She is organized and detailed; I am spontaneous and creative. These differences cause a little friction now and then, but they also blend together to give our marriage and our ministry a completion and breadth it could never have with me alone. In fact, my ministry would never have existed without Norma. I became a servant to her, and she became a servant to me. And both of us became servants of God. If I had my life to live over, I would still choose Norma above any other woman. We have loved and served each other for almost half a century, and we are more in love today than ever before.

Make the Promise

Promise your mate that you will work to overcome your self-ish tendencies. Promise that you will look to Christ as your mentor and model, and that like Him, you will make your life one of service. Promise that you will trust Christ for all your needs, knowing that putting yourself in His hands will free you to change your focus from your own concerns to your mate's. Promise your mate that you will make it your project to know his or her needs and dreams, and that you will dedicate yourself to meeting those needs and making those dreams come true.

Make this promise and your marriage will become solidly secure, bringing real joy to both of you. You will find that being a servant will make you happier than you have ever been.

EPILOGUE:
THE "I PROMISE" CONSTITUTION

Whether you are a couple who read this book together, a participant in a small group study, or an individual who read it alone, I hope what I've written has convinced you that making certain promises to your mate is highly valuable and crucial to establishing the security you desire for your marriage.

Any time you have more than one person engaged in a great undertaking, it's good to have specific understandings written on paper so that no one will be uncertain or confused about direction. That's why the founding fathers of our great nation wrote a constitution to guide the new government they were establishing. And history has shown us the enormous value of this document. The United States Constitution has guided the ship of state for more than two and a quarter centuries.

Marriage is an undertaking of untold importance. The home that lovers establish when they take their vows can affect not only time, but all of eternity. It is God's first earthly institution, the foundation of a stable society, and a source of untold potential for joy and fulfillment. So why shouldn't your marriage have a constitution?

I believe it should. That is why I have summarized the five promises I've presented in this book and put them in the form of a constitution—the "I Promise Constitution," as I've called it. This document gives you the opportunity to show your mate that your promises are not merely empty words that evaporate into the air the moment you speak them. Rather, you *mean* what you promise, and you are willing to have these promises written, signed, and dated to demonstrate your sincerity. So I urge you to sign your marriage constitution.

You can either adopt and sign the constitution as I have written it here, or use it as a guide for creating your own. If you use mine, just cut it from the book and place it where you and your mate can look at it any time to remind yourselves of what you have committed to do in order to provide security for your marriage.

I Promise
CONSTITUTION

Preamble: When we wed I committed to love and cherish you all the days of my life, and I affirm that commitment today. I love you dearly, more than life itself. I honor you and place you above all other people in my life. My goal is to create in our marriage a place of safety and security in which you and I can share everything without fear and grow together in deeper love and intimacy. To confirm my commitment to this goal, I willingly make these five solemn promises to you.

I Promise to conform my beliefs to God's truth. I will gain control of my outlook, emotions, and happiness by continually examining my deepest beliefs and striving to make them consistent with what God's Word says. I take sole responsibility for my beliefs with the understanding that they, not you, determine my emotions, expectations, and actions. Thus I lift from you the burden of being responsible for me.

I Promise to be filled by God. I will keep God in my heart as my source of joy and love. My love for you will be His love flowing through me. And I will receive your love as overflow from Him. I will base the security of our marriage on making Christ my Boss. I will strive to conform to His image and follow all His commands, especially the one to love you and care for you all the days of my life. (Ephesians 5:25–26; Philippians 4:19)

I Promise to find God's best in every trial. I give you the security of knowing that the negative things that happen in our marriage will not destroy my love for you. I will not expect perfection from you, but will use even the irritations between us as opportunities to see my blind spots and foster my personal growth. I will call on the power of Christ to root out my weaknesses. (Romans 8:28; James 1:12; Romans 5:3–5)

I Promise to listen and communicate with love. I will value every word you speak as a window to your heart. I will honor your opinions, feelings, needs, and beliefs so that you will feel free to speak honestly and openly with full security in my love for you. I will be open with you in communicating my heart and will consider your feelings and needs in all my words. (Ephesians 4:29)

I Promise to serve you all the days of my life. I will fight all tendencies toward selfishness in me and focus on keeping you, your needs, and your goals before me at all times. I will serve you willingly and wholeheartedly, just as Christ served His disciples not only in small, humble ways but also by giving His life for them and for us as well. (Galatians 5:13)

Signed: _____   Date: _____

Signed: _____   Date: _____

NOTES

Chapter One
1. Intense research by The National Marriage Institute on what helps couples stay in love determined that safety was the foundation to all satisfying and healthy marriages.
2. Genesis 2:24

Chapter Two
1. C.S. Lewis, *The Weight of Glory* (New York: Macmillan Publishing Company, 1949), 18, 19.
2. David Stoop, *You Are What You Think* (Grand Rapids: Fleming H. Revell, 1982, 1986), 31.

Chapter Three
1. Pat Love, *The Truth About Love.*

Chapter Four
1. Matthew McKay, Ph.D., Martha Davis, Ph.D, and Patrick Fanning, *Thoughts and Feelings* (Oakland, California: New Harbinger Publications, Inc., 1997), 19.
2. A.T. Beck, *Cognitive Therapy and the Emotional Disorders* (New York: Guilford Press, 1976), as quoted in McKay, Davis, and Fanning, *Thoughts and Feelings*, 19.

Chapter Five
1. Mace, D., & Mace, R. (1980). *Enriching Marriages: The Foundation Stone of Family Strength.* In N. Stinnett, B. Chesser, J. Defrain, & P. Knaub (Eds.), Family strengths: Positive models for family life (Lincoln, NE: University of Nebraska Press), 197–215.

Chapter Six

1. Doc Childre and Howard Martin, *The Heartmath Solution* (New York: Harper Collins, 1999), 115–117.

Chapter Seven

1. If sharing your feelings is difficult, you might find help in *The Language of Love* by Gary Smalley and John Trent. This book gives men a powerful method for communicating feelings, and women can use it to help men really understand them.

2. *The Language of Love* by Gary Smalley and John Trent, and *The DNA of Relationships*.

Smalley relationship CENTER

The Smalley Relationship Center provides conferences and resources for couples, singles, parents, and churches. The Center captures research, connecting to your practical needs and develops new tools for building relationships.

resources include:

- Over 40 best-selling books on relationships
- Small Group curriculums on marriage & parenting
- Church-wide campaign series with sermon series, daily emails and much more
- Video/DVD series
- Newlywed kit and pre-marital resources

www.garysmalley.com website includes:

- Over 300 articles on practical relationship topics
- Weekly key truths on practical issues
- Daily devotionals
- Conference dates and locations
- Special events
- Weekly newsletter
- Free personality & core fear profiles
- Request a SRC Speaker

To find out more about Gary Smalley's speaking schedule, conferences, and to receive a weekly e-letter with articles and coaching ideas on your relationships, go to www.garysmalley.com.

Attend our live **I Promise Marriage Seminars** taught by

DRS. GARY & GREG
SMALLEY

A six session marriage seminar based on the new
I Promise book and Purpose Driven Curriculum

4 Free Resources: go to www.garysmalley.com

1 • Video File
Watch Gary Smalley, in his own words in an interview style, answer six frequently asked questions about I Promise with a powerful summation of the key concepts.

2 • Profiles
The overall theme of I Promise is security, and you can take a 20 question test on how secure your most important relationship is. (Bonus: After you take that profile consider taking our personality profile which gives you even more insight into what kind of personality styles you and your spouse fall into.)

3 • Audio File
In this 45-minute streaming audio presentation, Gary Smalley shares his latest I Promise insights with Rick Warren's Purpose-Driven staff at the headquarters in Lake Forest, California.

4 • Weekly E-letter
Receive articles, coaching tips and, inspirational encouragement from Gary Smalley which will help you build a more effective and stronger marriage.

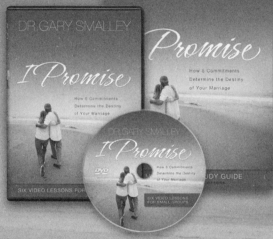